WHISPERS OF GHOSTS

Also by Greg Dinner

A Murmuration of Starlings
Narcissus In Utero
A Requiem For Hania

WHISPERS OF GHOSTS

A Journal of Days and Nights
Ukraine

Greg Dinner

Copyright © 2024 by Greg Dinner
All rights reserved

Dinner, Greg.
Whispers of Ghosts: A Journal of Days and Nights Ukraine
/ Greg Dinner

'The End and the Beginning' © Wisława Szymborska
Trans by Joanna Trzeciak   Used by permission

'Funeral Blues' © W.H. Auden
Used by permission

For further information contact
Ogham & Dabar Books
Kilrateera
Mountshannon
Country Clare
Republic of Ireland
V94 H9YN
Visit: **www.gregdinner.com**

ISBN:
9781737774341

Printed by Ingram Spark

Greg Dinner has asserted his moral rights under the Copyright, Designs and Patents Act UK, 1988, to be identified as the author of this work.

All rights reserved. This book is copyright material and must not be copied, reproduced, distributed, leased, licensed or publish performed or used in any way except as specifically permitted by the publisher.

This is a work of non fiction. All observations, comments, opinions, remarks and references are of the author alone. This book is not to be distributed unless permission of the publisher is granted.

Cover photograph ©Greg Dinner 2024

In Memory of Victoria Amelina
and Vladimir Vakulenko

From a Facebook post by PEN Ukraine:

"March 24 is the day of death of Vladimir Vakulenko-k, a Ukrainian writer who was killed by Russian occupiers.

During the occupation Vladimir left a diary that later found our dear Victoria Amelina. These are painful and true records, which led the writer from the beginning of the full-scale invasion all the way to his own abduction by occupiers in the native village of Kapitolívka szyums bokogo district, in Kharkiv region, March 24, 2022.

The day before the kidnapping, he hid a diary under a cherry tree, commanding his father, 'When ours come - give it back.' Already after the release of Kapitolívka on September 24, 2022, a diary in the yard of Vakulenkív found writer Victoria Amelina together with Vladimir's father.

The last entry in the diary, which has 36 pages, was made by Vladimir on March 21, 2022. 'Everything will be Ukraine! I believe in victory,'-written by hand in a notebook in a cell."

Ukrainian PEN, publishing house Vivat and Харківський ЛітМузей published Vakulenko's diary supported by Міжнародний фонд "Відродження". The copy of the edition was completely bought out twice."

Foreword

The following records events and emotions from a visit first to Krakow in February, 2024, and mostly then in the continuation of this journey in February and March that took me along the length of Ukraine, a country very much at war, beneath the watchful eyes, mostly, of PEN Ukraine, a sister PEN member to my own PEN Ireland.

Almost all of these diary entries focus on my travels and days in Ukraine. However whilst the time spent in Krakow was for research purposes of the novel I am working on, *Fragments*, it felt necessary to begin these recollections there, and during one day in particular.

In Krakow I spent much of my time wandering the Jewish area of Kazimierz, visiting the old synagogues, graveyards, staring at the buildings, the past. This however is largely on the 'tourist trail.' In the many golf cart-like carriers that drive down the old streets, the guides tell the story of the area and its former denizens, most of whom were killed in the Holocaust; those stories I need not repeat.

There was one place, however, that the carts do not go, that tourists do not visit, but that was central to my time in Krakow. That I needed to witness, and know, and return, and feel.

The Babinski Institute in Kobierzyn is about forty minutes from the centre of Krakow by tram. Now Kobierzyn is a suburb of the main city; back in the 1930s, the 1940s, it was more its own village: connected but distinct. It was, and is, the site of the Krakow mental hospital. Whilst still somewhat in use today, its functions are not as central to its history as they once were. Now in many ways it is a public park, whilst some of its many buildings remain in use as a hospital.

The Institute is quite central in the fictional story of *A Requiem For Hania*. Here, fictionally, the then self-imposed silent Hannah Kielar, whose background and identity are largely unrevealed, falls under the care of Dr. Kazimierz Palinsky. And in turn, he falls under her warmth, her honesty, her amused eye, which is to say he falls deeply in love with her without ever knowing the truth of her background.

The Institute also plays a central story in one of the sections of *Fragments*. In this new work, the story focuses on the fictionalized version of the real-life patient, Waleria 'Lera' Białońska. I had long been aware of Białońska's story; I had felt it important to tell her story as I wished to imagine it in *Fragments;* indeed it remains central to the reason for developing this new book.

My motivations for entering Ukraine were not the same as those for spending time in Krakow. And yet Krakow, and particularly Kobierzyn, are both part of the same story as Ukraine, the same journey. That journey in fact begins at the Institute.

I went to Kobierzyn to bear witness, to see where my fictional 'Lera' lived, and survived. The real Waleria Białońska, not Jewish, also survived: she was the only patient at the Institute who did.

Almost a year before the events of 1942, most of the Jewish patients had been removed to an hospital close to Warsaw, in Otwock. It too plays a part in *A Requiem For Hania*, and a very minor appearance in *Fragments.* I had been to Otwock two years earlier, but I had not had the chance yet to visit Kobierzyn. It was here, in 1941, that the Jewish patients were taken from the hospital to a facility in the North, and eventually to Treblinka. The non-Jewish patients at the Babinski Institute remained, until they were sent to another death camp, to Auschwitz, and there to extermination: defined by their murderers as deficient misfits who had no place in the Nazi Reich.

The SS arrived at the Babinski Institute on the morning of 22 June, 1942, to take the remaining patients to cattle cars waiting for them. The hospital's Nazi director, Alex Kroll helped oversee the operation. Those patients too elderly and too ill to move were liquidated—some by euthanasia injection, some shot where they lay.

Waleria however, had worked as a maid for Norbert Chmielewski, head of the hospital office. Chmielewski was desperate to save Waleria and enlisted the help of a nurse, Stanisława Pałys, who had a great fondness for the girl. When the SS arrived, Nurse Pałys hid Waleria behind a large wardrobe, then that night helped her to climb out of the 2nd floor window and finally to escape to a local farmer after the SS had gone.

No other patient would survive the exterminations.

My time at Kobierzyn was, in truth, part of my journey to bear witness: to events of the past, and to events of the present. What I discovered there I had not expected to find; it too was a deeply involving and humbling experience. For this reason, that event, that morning, is included as the starting point for my journey. And my search.

*

The first part of these reminisces and observations are largely a journal of events—mostly the wheres and whens. Generally these are factual. Despite its largely present tense narrative the journal here was written after the fact, so that I would remember, especially at a time when memory sometimes fades with age.

There are some things I need to remember.

The second part, however, often coincides, crossing over the first, repeating. These are my immediate thoughts of the day, less a journal of events than an emotional journal or diary: what I felt about certain things I did, how such touched me, deeply. And sometimes hurt. Arguably this is more important, and valuable, to me as a writer and a person than the simple diary that is Part I. At times these entries therefore cross over to say the same things. That is by necessity. But the purposes of their recording were, and are, quite different.

I need to remember what I saw, where I went, what was revealed.

But I also need to remember what I felt. And feel still. Some things do not alter with time.

The final two parts of the book include two letters—one open, one to some family members, both of which I felt were relevant to the journey undergone. The last part is an afterword. Because the ghosts still whisper in my ear. Because some images remain.

I suspect the whisperings will always be with me. Some things I will likely forget. The purpose of these reminisces is so that, as I grow old, I might not.

About some things I will not need reminding, I will not forget. Those whisperings remain with me as I wake and as I sleep. Those images I hold dear as well.

Those words, those moments, will remain. And so it should be.

I.

A Diary of Days and Nights

"There are things in us that we can find again only by going back."
Pascal Mercier *Night Train To Lisbon*,
whispered in *A Requiem for Hania*

I have taken a journey. A journey of heart and mind.

I first took trains from London to Ludwigsburg in western Germany in order to break bread and spend the night with some dear German friends: Jasmin, a woman born Palestinian, her lovely husband Felix and their infant son Junes, and a common friend Inga, a 'media architect', the daughter of the one-time German ambassador to the United States, whose aristocratic background belies her down-to-earth warmth and intelligence. It was important for me to stop with them in this awful time of the Gaza war, with what is happening to the Palestinians following the horrific Hamas attack on Israel, but also at a time of great antisemitism, particularly elevated and hurtful in Ireland. I needed to see them, to hold out my hand of friendship. I need not have been worried. Events at large cannot diminish the mutual respect and kindness we all share.

From Ludwigsburg I travelled on trains through Munich and Vienna to Krakow, here to spend a few days research on the book *Fragments*, the fictional offshoot/journey I write now as a follow-on to my previous novel *A Requiem For Hania*.

For the most part, this record herewith is not where I had intended recording my thoughts and memories concerning those research days in Krakow, important and invaluable as they were. However I realized the experience there both confirmed and developed the broader journey that followed and the ideas that formed and began to find voice within.

In particular a morning wandering around the grounds and buildings of the Babinski Institute, Kobierzyn, whilst not the beginning of my journey into Ukraine, seem to me to be very much a part of the journey I would undertake. So my first diary entry begins there—walking in the shadow of the real-life Waleria Białońska, who I fictionalize but remember in this new work in progress, *Fragments*. Like so many of the ghosts who would begin to haunt me in Ukraine, and after, Waleria—Lera—too haunts. Thus it seems most appropriate that I begin the diary with her story, and those whisperings that I continue to hear in the depth of night.

When I left Krakow a couple days later, I took a train to the near Ukraine Polish border town of Przemyśl, and from there this journal finds its true beginning. It records my movements and days in Ukraine, a country at war for almost two years to the day, a country that 'begins' where *Fragments* will end…and a country and its people that will burn deeply in my memories, and my heart.

What follows is a diary of events. At the end of this first part I will reproduce a second record: the impressions and emotional minefield of what was felt that I first put largely on social media. Rather than a record of events, I set these thoughts down daily so that others might know how it was, not just what it was. Or perhaps so I would remember; memory is important to me. I fear the forgetting.

That second part, and indeed the two remaining sections, should be seen as companions to the first. There are times when it is necessary to remember emotional travels as well as travels of place.

This was not 'the journey', one with a beginning and ending; it is instead part of a larger journey, likely without end. The journey of one who is now old, and in perhaps a final albeit long road still-to-travel phase. So that I do not forget. So that words might outlive.

Thus the going forward.
And the coming back.

2 March 2024

There is somewhere I need to go, well in the south of Krakow city. A friend's friend agrees to take me there, as it is not always easy to navigate the tram and bus system for me. To act as guide, up to a point. I have no idea what awaits and thought I could use help for this part of the research I want to do.

The tram goes one way—the wrong way it turns out, to the end of its run, where we have to descend…only to reascend the same waiting tram ten minutes after and go in the opposite direction. A Polish joke.

Thirty or forty minutes later we come to the end of the line in the former village, now suburb, of Kobierzyn. My 'guide' gets instructions from a driver and a local, and we wait for a bus with knowledge now of where to get off for the Babinski Institute.

When we descend the bus steps, on one side of the carriageway is a Kentucky Fried Chicken. A long, long way from the dark days of 1941 and 1942. We walk along the road to an entrance, and here turn into the long drive and grounds of the Babinski Institute Mental Hospital.

The Babinksi Institute was thriving back in the 1930s, 1940s. It is spread up a hill and consists of many buildings—residences, a canteen, a chapel, a theatre. All this I knew from the research I had done for the last few years. Now it is run down, visited as a park to stroll or exercise in. Some of the buildings, the units, are still used as a mental hospital, but despite its history, it has been mostly left to ghosts. There are patients and clinics still, but all is a shadow of what it was, once. Then. And what happened here, once. Then.

At the entrance, perhaps one hundred fifty meters away, there is sight of the first building, a gatehouse of sorts, farm building of sorts. I know what happened here on 22 June, 1942. I know that in this building, in the small upstairs flat within, Norbert Chmielewski, the head of the hospital office, was told to stay whilst the remaining six hundred or so patients were ushered from their rooms and quarters, to be escorted to waiting cattle cars at the nearby train siding, and ultimately to Auschwitz. Chmeilewski sits in the attic of this building watching events unfold. There is a phone line into it and he is told to wait for any communication from, or to, Nazi administrator Alex Kroll, largely responsible for all that would happen—and never punished for such. No call will ever come.

I stare at the building as we walk near, then up the hill of the main drive, to its roundabout entrance, the real entrance of the Institute, now empty. Here I know is the theatre building. Here patient musicians, a small orchestra, once practiced their song. All is silent now.

We glance at the many buildings to the right and left, most looking abandoned. A few cars. A few people walking in the distance. And us. My 'guide' accompanies me, but knows nothing of this place. Knowledge and memory are mine.

We walk for a long time, up one side, staring at some of the two and three story chalet buildings. Their secrets are largely long gone. We eventually make it to the back of the property, where a long hill slopes down, farmland. I have seen photographs of this place. This land. It has not much changed from the 1940s, in many ways. There are ghosts here, but perhaps I alone see them. Hear them.

At one building a window opens and someone stares at us. My guide asks for information, but the attendant has no answers. He suggests we go to the reception building. I had written to them once to make certain it is permissible to walk on the grounds, explore. I never received an answer in reply, unsurprisingly. I have no desire to go there now.

We continue walking, and after a while I find what I am looking for, what I knew existed from research. In the back of a building, nearly hidden, is a memorial to all that happened here. Actually there are three tied memorials A cross at the centre. On one side the names of all the patients who had been transported on that day in 1942, with words of memory in Polish. But on the other side, staring at it, are the names of the Jews who had been at the Institute. All had been forced to leave in the autumn of 1941, taken to Otwock near Warsaw, to the hospital there. And from there, in 1942, they were taken to Treblinka.

And murdered in the gas chamber.

I had been to Otwock. It too features somewhat in *A Requiem For Hania*. It too is about ghosts.

I stare at the monument to the Jewish patients, in Hebrew and Polish. A list of names, surnames that I understand even if I do not always know the lettering. I know them. They are names I grew up with. Jewish surnames.

I finds some stones to leave at the foot of the monument, as is our way. I say, quietly, kaddish, to remember. No one visits here any longer. Few remember. I do. I know the story. I use it for fiction. But the facts always hold more weight than fiction. That weight of water. Thus I remember and witness.

From there we stroll, staring at other buildings, until we come to one dilapidated 'chalet', abandoned, some protective fencing around much of it. Unseen, we try the door, find it unlocked.

Much of a ruin inside, but something I wanted, and needed to see. We wander from room to room, amidst broken glass, plaster and filth on the floor. Rooms of the mad. Quarters of the ill. We enter an old bath and toilet area, with only bits of pipework, shower and bath works showing. In another room, an old gurney, rusted and falling apart. Some old bed frames. Upstairs more of the same.

You can picture what went on here. And what happened. Thick with atmosphere and memory.

Thick with confusion of patients. Thick too with the nurses and sisters and doctors who once roamed the corridors.

And the tears. And the fear. Fear weighs on water.

Those patients who could not be taken away by the SS were euthanized on the day. Kroll did some of the injecting. Others were shot in the head, dying too in silence. Did it happen here? In this place? Does anyone remember, or am I alone?

I sense that I am alone.

We walk through the building, dilapidated room beside destroyed, old room. I know. In *Fragments* an imagined literary-created patient here leaves an old trunk, with a broken violin hidden within. The trunk: not an imagined image but one such I had seen in photographs of this place. I do not find it now, that trunk, that broken violin, but it is here, in my imagination if not in the reality.

So I know this place, both real and recreated in the pages of my literary odyssey. I know what happened here, in truth, those dark days of June 1942. I know. I can see it then. I can see it now.

In silence we leave this building and walk, heading back in the direction of the entrance. I note what is the reception building that is now active for the little of the hospital that remains, and functions as such. Cars are parked there. An ambulance. But they can tell me nothing and we do not walk in that direction.

Instead we head towards a small central building, clearly the chapel for the Institute, then and now. I walk up the stairs of the covered portico, but the front door is locked. However what I find on the walls of the portico both astonishes me and touches me deeply.

Here, on one side, a plaque in memory of Waleria Białońska, she alone of the patients who survived this place. She who I have been writing about, as my fictional 'Lera' based on Waleria's story. Lera's fictional love story for a young man, and love too for an old man. A fictional story that touches me deeply, even as the true story, which I well know, touches me deeply.

Here Waleria's name in bronze. Does anyone really remember her as I do now? Does anyone really know her, still, as I do now? I stare at this plaque, wide-eyed to have found it. The ghosts really do speak, and laugh at us.

On the other side of the portico, another plaque. This one is to the nurse who saved Waleria, Stanisława Pałys, the duty nurse at the time who hid Waleria behind a clothes wardrobe, then that night helped her to climb out from the building, telling her to run to a farmer Stanisława Pałys knew.

This story too is part of *Fragments*, fictionalized but to me very real.

I stare at the copper plate memories, speaking to me now. I remember. I hardly know the words to say. But I am touched, amazed, close to tears. Their stories move me and moved me. I take these two women with me. I am one of the last of a generation who will probably remember.

I back away in silence. It is hard to know how to respond. I take some obligatory photos, although the chapel, the hospital are burned now into memory.

We walk back towards the theatre building, then down the long drive. I can see what happened here, eighty-two years ago. I can see Waleria as she was, and as I created. My Lera.

We say nothing as we leave here. It is not that it confirmed what I knew, what I then imagined. It is that I have been here now as well as being here in my imagination. I have seen the worst. I have seen the loss. And I have seen a little hope in a woman who did not die. And who did not die for me.

It is the beginning of the journey I will take; I know that now. Necessary. It always was, but now, more than ever, it is the start of what I must do.

I take a last glance at the hospital grounds, disappearing into trees and fenced in memories.

I am here.
I am not here.

I begin.

<u>4 March</u>

I catch an old Ukrainian/Soviet train from Przemyśl in Poland, near the border with Ukraine, to Lviv.

In my 'cabin' are two others. Yulia studied law in Lviv and now works as a paralegal in Bristol. She is a lovely young woman from Ivano-Frankivsk. I tell her I will be going there and we arrange to meet for coffee. She acts as translator for me with Valery, also with us for the journey. Valery speaks some Spanish and we trade comments in such, but mostly it is English and Ukrainian.

Valery is in the army. He is 59. He has been on leave for two weeks, now heading back. His hope is that at 60 he will retire. He mentions his son, in his thirties, who has just been called up into the reserves. Valery is not happy about it. Isn't one from the family enough? His son has his own family, a business with people working for him. Children. Responsibilities. It should not be like this.

They learn I am a writer and I show them a copy of *Hania*; I have a number with me to give away, but not enough to gift now. Valery says he too wants to leave something behind when he dies. He wishes he could write, for example. I try to tell him that what matters, what he leaves behind, is what he will give to his grandchildren. That is what matters. That is passed on. Don't die, I want to say. Do not die…

Arrivals in Lviv. I am met by poet Iya Kiva. Lovely woman. Her English is fairly good. She will take me to the hotel. We are meeting for a funny reason. I had read on facebook her comments about the war and Ivano Frankivsk when she was reading her poems there, so sent a message that I would love to meet if she had time. But she never saw the message. On my way to Krakow, the train from Munich to Vienna, I am about thirty minutes outside of Vienna when I see a facebook comment from her: if anyone will be in Vienna, she needs a small thing brought to Lviv. I respond that I will be in Vienna in thirty minutes, transferring for one hour, if she can get whatever it is to me. She has no idea who I am, but what she needs is a prepaid train ticket from a ticket machine. I offer to collect it for her—do—and I carry it to Lviv with me.

So we meet in order that I can hand over the ticket. I give her a copy of *Hania*. I had not intended to, but somehow it seems necessary. She is lovely. I hope to meet her again in Kyiv, where she is heading. She is going to give a reading of her poetry at the PEN Ukraine space. I tell her I will be there and plan to attend. She says it will be in Ukrainian. I tell her it does not matter: I will understand by sound, by gesture, from the audience. I would like to attend. That is the plan. In fact the need.

I am staying at the George Hotel, recommended by Philippe Sands. Definitely is a funny place, as he promised: a bit Wes Anderson, a bit old school. But I rather like it. It is comfortable, right in the centre of Lviv. It has a bomb shelter, they tell me. I do not intend to use it. A hotel like this will last forever. As good as any Hollywood location, missing only the obligatory bellboy. Perhaps next time.

5 March

After getting my Vodaphone sim so I have access to internet whilst travelling—at least sometimes—I make my way to what I thought was the cultural centre. In fact it is the Centre for Urban History. The head of the centre, Sofia Dyak, had spoken two years ago at a conference in Warsaw I attended, centred around the exhibition put together by Natalia Romek. I have been in contact with Natalia; quietly, unknowingly, a character based on her plays a central role in *Fragments* that I am now writing. Sofia Dyak is out of town but I meet instead with Maryana Mazurak, deputy director, and Taras Nazaruk who does research and events at the centre. Both are very kind, very helpful. I knew that Philippe Sands had also had help with his work there, and attended a conference held by them, so I discuss my particular interest in Lviv during the Holocaust years. Maryana and Taras give me a great deal of information, and some internet links to look at. I tell them I will bring a copy of *Hania* for their library, which they seemed to appreciate. I do so the following day; it is a book that haunts a number of libraries. That pleases me.

I spend the rest of the day wandering (and getting lost) in Lviv, exploring what was once the ghetto. I know of the Chiger group, who lived in the sewers hiding from the Nazis, thanks to Maryana and Taras: now I walk along the Chigers' route, above ground, just where they had rested below for years. The trams above, the large church square, people passing by. Do they know? Do they remember. I remember. A tram passes.

And the borders of what was the ghetto, long since disappeared.

Too late to go to the Janowska camp, now a prison. Too late to stop by the small stone memorial across from it, overlooking the ravine where the thousands of Lviv Jews were shot and dumped, later then burned. Too late to pay my respects, my silent words. Silent prayer of remembrance.

So I walk to the Law Faculty where Raphael Lemkin and Hersch Lauterpacht, who later would come to define both Crimes Against

Humanity and importantly Genocide at Nuremberg, had studied and taught. Philippe Sands tells the story brilliantly in *East West Street*. His to tell, not mine. But here I stand staring for a long moment; I think, I remember. And I wonder how to respond to the situation in Gaza, troubling to me so? I wonder how to understand my own wanderings? I wonder without answers. Needs, feelings, but no real answers.

Most of the time, I simply wander.

I am alone for dinner. Some messages confused, and I do not realize that three writers are waiting for me elsewhere. I will meet one the following day, and meet another in Kyiv. Both of them will affect me greatly.

6 March

I have arranged to meet writer and PEN member Sofia Cheliak at the entrance to the Lychakiv Cemetery. The walk there from the hotel takes about twenty minutes. In slight drizzle I stand outside one gate, keeping an eye on the correct open gate down the block. The cemetery reminds of Pere LaChaise in Paris…same fascinating crypts. Just minus the internationally known names and crypt sculptures, and the cats. And an Oscar Wilde gravestone with the Jacob Epstein sculpted testicles chipped away. To each his own souvenir.

As I wait a cortege comes towards me from the opposite direction. It does not pass into the cemetery. I learn later it is bringing a fallen soldier to the funeral home. I watch as all cars stop. People get out of their cars, stand at attention, showing respect…cars in both directions, people on the streets. Another young soldier martyred, a true hero to these people. But there is no joy, only respect. A sense of loss. I share that sense.

They are losing a generation of young people. The 'new' lost generation. Lost in too many ways.

I see Sofia heading towards me; easy to recognize. We meet at the gate to the cemetery and she takes me in. She explains that the city council had not allowed Victoria Amelina to be buried in the martyrs' area, as she was not a soldier.

Victoria Amelina meant something to me; a lot actually. Although I never met her, we had exchanged messages. She had been at a concert for Ukraine in Dublin where we were to meet. I had wanted to give her a copy of *A Requiem For Hania*. I had followed her work for the previous eighteen months or so, and I felt a strong kinship to a writer who also felt it imperative to bear witness: in her case to the devastation and loss in her own country. She had travelled the length and breadth taking witness statements, finding missing journals written by Ukrainian writers, becoming a spokeswoman for the cause: mostly for those lost, for the destruction she witnessed. She was, emotionally, a mentor, a heroine, a belief. A need. But at the concert there were too many people and we missed each other. I subsequently gave *Hania* to a colleague who was to get it to her by post and other means.

In what I guessed would have been just when Victoria might have received my gift, word came that she had been in a pizza restaurant with two South American journalists in Kramatorsk exactly as a Russian missile struck. Victoria died a couple days later, never regaining consciousness. I was emotionally devastated. It is very hard to explain this to people but it left an emotional vacuum within. What she was doing, what I feel I need to do now, remains as kin. Victoria was, will always be, my sister.

Sofia leads me to her grave, not far from the entrance, crowded between a couple others. Because Victoria has only been buried for eight months or so, the mound is still there, somewhat fresh, the final gravestone not yet laid. Instead there is a cross at the head of the grave, and many flowers resting on the dirt with messages. By the cross is a stuffed unicorn: she loved unicorns.

We stand there for a long time, thinking. I lay some flowers I had bought on the grave; these I had in my thoughts purchased on behalf of PEN Ireland colleagues who at one time I felt offered support to me let alone Victoria. With the very real upsurge of antisemitism in Ireland, which I now keenly feel, I am not quite so certain; I am deeply troubled by this.

After laying the flowers, I ask Sofia, if appropriate, if I might say a poem. Thus I recite 'Funeral Blues', altered to the feminine, by WH Auden:

Stop all the clocks, cut off the telephone,
Prevent the dog from barking with a juicy bone,
Silence the pianos and with muffled drum
Bring out the coffin, let the mourners come.

Let aeroplanes circle moaning overhead
Scribbling on the sky the message 'She is Dead'.
Put crepe bows round the white necks of the public doves,
Let the traffic policemen wear black cotton gloves.

She was my North, my South, my East and West,
My working week and my Sunday rest,
My noon, my midnight, my talk, my song;
I thought that love would last forever: I was wrong.

The stars are not wanted now; put out every one,
Pack up the moon and dismantle the sun,
Pour away the ocean and sweep up the wood;
For nothing now can ever come to any good.

The poem has always touched me and I felt it suited to my thoughts. I changed the gender to reflect Victoria. It was later told to me that Auden wrote the poem with irony. Perhaps. But nevertheless the poem touches me and as such I am pleased I had chosen it to recite at the graveside.

I then ask my friend Sofia, with tears in her eyes, again if it was appropriate that I would like to lay a stone, and to say kaddish. I explain that this is the way of my people. Sofia is certain Victora would have liked this. Thus Kaddish is said in Hebrew, and a stone placed at the grave. Sofia wanted me to place it beside the unicorn at its head.

I later write to my PEN Ireland colleagues to explain. This is what I write to them:

Today, beneath a weeping grey sky, on behalf of PEN Ireland I placed flowers on the grave of Victoria Amelina.

For Pen Ireland, Victoria is now an empty chair. A memory. On behalf of PEN Ireland, therefore, I placed flowers. And remembered her. And saw the ghost of her smile before me.

For me, however, Victoria was something more. She was one who bore witness, just as it has been my life's work to bear witness. In that I was connected: the need to remember. The need to know. The need to tell a story. On behalf then of myself I recited the poem below, slightly adapted. It is a poem that has always touched me, and meant something to me.

On behalf of myself, too, I placed a small stone I carried from Ireland at the head of her grave, joining the unicorns that I'm told she loved so.

And I said Kaddish, which I was told would have in fact pleased her. I think few, if any of you, will understand the meaning of that. So following the poem below, I will quote from A Requiem For Hania as explanation.

From *A Requiem For Hania*

"There was a second request. Pawel, like so many of us, had been to so many funerals over the years, particularly these last years. Thus, the nature of growing old. That is never easy. He said his other request was that we today say Kaddish for him, the Mourner's Kaddish at his passing. Kaddish in the Jewish liturgy has been said for a thousand years. It is a prayer that praises God. But it also is a prayer to honour the deceased. It reflects on life itself. On tradition. And most of all I think for Pawel it reflects on family. To say Kaddish is an act of kindness. An act of remembrance."

"Pawel's lovely Warsaw family told me how they had visited their mother's grave with Pawel, an act of remembrance. Of thanksgiving for them and for him. Agnieszka told me quietly how touched she was when Pawel left a stone he had picked up at Treblinka days earlier, how he placed this stone on her Grandmother's headstone. I explained to her, as Pawel would have known, that this is part of our tradition. For us, we do not leave flowers, as flowers are temporal. Rather we leave small stones at a grave. Those stones that we place on a headstone or nearby suggest that we are all of the earth, where life is short and long at the same time. The stones say we remember all our lives and beyond. That we were there and that the loss of a loved one will be part of our memories forever."

I have come here as an Other so as to voice my support, my respect, my hope and belief in the humanity of these gracious people. And I reflect that in Ireland, these last five months, such like voice in my ears has grown painfully silent.

I will now travel the length of Ukraine, often accompanied by my friends here from PEN Ukraine. I will offer to them my embrace, my words, my voice. And I will bear witness.

To all of you, I send regards
Greg Dinner

No one from Irish PEN responded.

*

With both of us emotional, Sofia slightly in tears, we leave the graveyard. I learn later why Sofia was so moved. Victoria had once gone to New York and returned with a gift for her friend: poetry of American poet Allen Ginsburg. The poem 'Kaddish'.

Sofia had translated Ginsburg's poem from English to Ukrainian, but has never actually heard Kaddish read in Hebrew, as a prayer of remembrance.

Now she had heard.

And Kaddish… was said.

*

We decide to go to a nearby restaurant for lunch, very much a Ukrainian affair. We stay for some time, chatting.

Later Sofia takes me to an institute she thought I would find interesting to meet people there; only when arriving do I discover that it is the same institute, as well as then its correct name, The Institute of European Studies. We laugh that I had been there before. I leave my book as a gift as I had promised, and walk. It is enough for me.

That night I dine alone. It feels the right way to leave the city.

7-9 March
Ivano Frankivsk

These days a blur. The three hour train ride south towards the Carpathian Mountains in the direction of Moldova. I get a 'Bolt' cab to take me to the appointed hotel, a bit Holiday Inn-ish, on the other side of this small, Austro-Hungarian City. It is a pretty, fairly modern city. Or perhaps the word is undamaged. The Soviets had named is Stanislav; the Ukrainians recaptured its name. And its identity.

PEN Ukraine has arranged the hotel room for me. More of a suite with a sort of four poster bed ninety degrees to the rest of the room. I leave my bags, decide to walk to the meeting place for the young writers' festival taking place, sponsored by PEN Ukraine and others, including the US Embassy and the British Council.

The walk takes me along a large lake across from the hotel, then through the main park that seems to dominate the city. A pretty place, quiet now as it is winter still. Then down a main avenue with its Vienna-like buildings, tidy, and I could be anywhere in Europe. The Austro-Hungarian influence, faded but still in evidence.

The Promprylad/Renovations Festival is held in a building that had been a converted warehouse or factory, with the entire community coming and going. There are a dozen or so small restaurants on the ground floor, from sushi and pizza to sandwiches to Ukrainian cuisine. I walk in and immediately spot Tetyana Teren, the vice president of PEN Ukraine and one of my hosts, having lunch. She is with Alyssa Bondareko who organized the festival, and another PEN media officer, Hannah Ustynova. They all helped organize my visit…in so many words allowed it, and thus willing to put up with my nonsense.

A bit later I am taken to the third floor of what in some ways is a media type centre, but in others just glassed office/rooms where various art-led companies work. The festival works out of one large conference area in the centre of it all, where the sixteen (reduced to fifteen) students or young people have workshops, conferences, discussions.

I am first introduced to the 'curator' of the festival, Ostap Slyvynsky. I immediately take to Ostap, a thoughtful, incredibly talented poet/writer. When the war broke out, he found he could no longer harness words. Words escaped him. So he went to the Lviv central train station—he is from Lviv—and began taking testimonies from refugees pouring in. These testimonies made their way into a book he wrote, 'The Dictionary of War'…Alphabetized testimony, both fiction and non, of what it means to be a war refugee, of the need to talk, to tell a story, to try to make people understand. The book is not yet in English, but will be at the end of the year. It is a purchase I am eager to make. And read.

Ostap is a delight. Like everyone, younger than I am, but he could be a mentor, or a friend. I am drawn to his thoughtfulness…

The young writers begin to wander in from lunch and I sit in the back away from their large horse-shoe table, with a large screen before them. I had wanted to spend time with these young people, hearing their stories, finding out what young people here seek to know, what they write about now, dream about for the future. I had wanted to remain relatively anonymous, but PEN wanted me introduced, a bit more forward. I soon learned why: so few come from outside Ukraine, showing support, showing they care, that I was an anomaly. And a curiosity. I had thought some Scottish writers would be there, even if the few Americans involved would be so on screens, but I was wrong. All English language folk stayed home, communicated over zoom for sessions. I was the only one there who came from western Europe— excepting a Canadian guy in the venue I met one afternoon who was there teaching English and walking the world from Ivano Frankivsk; everyone else stays away. Safety concerns. That I get. Down in Ivano Frankivsk the risks are minimal, but I do understand, although the loss of real contact is indeed a loss for all parties.

So I am introduced to the young people, who look at me a bit oddly, but appreciatively. They will become more so later. As will I. There are fifteen 'students' in all…mostly young women in their twenties, perhaps four or five young men. And as I will learn, they are all young professionals at their craft, their talent, their art: all wonderful writers.

That afternoon's session includes some Americans talking/ working with the students over zoom—asking questions, speaking or doing a remote workshop. Poet/novelist Rachel DeWoskin, speaking from Chicago, speaks a bit too fast, like a New Yorker (where I thought she might be from,) but is terrific with the students. I am impressed with her work. She does a poetry workshop with them, gets them to write a poem while she waits. The results are fascinating. And good. Incredibly good. Rachel is generous with her time, and her spirit.

And in passing, the following day US writer Christopher Merrill, now head of the fantastic writing program at the University of Iowa, talks about bearing witness. He has worked in many war zones, and much of the work he has done as journalist and writer has been about bearing witness. I write to him to tell him how great I think his presentation was. He responds sometime later, noting that indeed we are kindred spirits. I wish I could meet him, talk to him; perhaps one day I will. He is terrific when he talks to these young people about his own experiences…and with so much support for Ukraine now wavering and diminishing in Congress. I do not want to comment on that to the young people. They will know anyway. Too many war weary out there. Here, you cannot be weary; you need to fight to survive. Too few beyond the borders, particularly in the US, understand what really is an existential war. And just exactly what that means.

Later I take a Bolt car back to the hotel after eating some sort of sandwich. I am slightly isolated, but determined to break ice with the young writers.

This I do on the following morning. It is after all a process.

I come downstairs to the café for breakfast. I see some young writers sitting together and pretty much force my way to their table, to sit, to talk, to explore, to find out about them. Who they are? Where do they come from? Why have they come here? Why? Part of the pre-requisite for the festival is that the young writers have to speak English, so they all do, well. They look surprised at first, but then pleased that I would make the effort—and so respond.

And we talk amidst mouthfuls: who they are. Where they grew up. What form they write in. Why it is important to them. What they are getting out of it. Sometimes who I am (I will always be known as Irish, never American.) Basically, what it means to be young, in war, where they will go in the world, how they will make their mark…

I later take a Bolt to the media centre. And much will become confused in my memory as to what happened when. I sit in on group discussions often in Ukrainian, but that does not matter. I am after reactions, expressions, the sounds of things even if I do not understand the words. As I will say over and over, the music even if I cannot understand the song.

Over time I befriend the students, best I can. It is impossible to say who I spoke to when, or names—usually, not always, an Iryna or Katherina or or…I befriend as many as I can on facebook. Facebook is the currency, the voice, the communication…that and Facebook Messenger. I quickly grasp it will be essential.

But I hear stories, sit at lunch with young people, enjoy their company in ways they would not know: the elderly latching on, perhaps leeching on, to the young. Vampire-like I need their youth to survive, their energy, talent, hope, despair. Faith. Them.

All who I meet are brilliant. The young women are usually the best talkers; no surprise there. The young men quieter. But I understand those young men are more likely at risk at the future. With the young women I could say come visit us in Ireland. They can come and go from Ukraine. Not so the young men, their futures more uncertain. More at risk.

I think to myself it is possible some of these young people might die in a war they do not want.

And this really pains. Gut wrenching pain.

Over the course of the time there I sit in on readings, events, various sessions. I listen to the wonderful Christopher Merrill, and sit in awe at a session of poetry in which four young Ukrainian poets had worked with four poets/academics in Scotland, online, translating two poems from each into their respective languages. One of the Scottish poets wrote in Scottish Gaelic, but English is the 'bridge' language. At this final session, held on the large screen via zoom for the young writers, all the poems are read in Ukrainian and in English (other than the two Gaelic poems,) eight poems in all. It is a most remarkable event, highlighting how language, and translation, transcends the words themselves into meaning, and music, and indeed poetry. I am completely blown away.

I also was asked, and agreed, to partake in one event I think will be a q&a, but it ends up being a talk. Every evening a film was shown, and whilst I was there they screened Michael Winterbottom's '24 Hour Party People'. Now I have met Michael; his Revolution Films' partner and producer Andrew Eaton once worked for me, now almost forty years previous. So I said I would be happy to discuss this film, although I am not particularly fond of it.

All the films were curated by the delightful Roman Malynovksy, a true cineaste. After the film is screened in Ukrainian (without subtitles) I cannot help but think that Steve Coogan is just not quite the same when dubbed; neither are the other actors, particularly Andy Serkis who really is very funny in the film. There is meant to be a q&a

then as I was used to. However as I said it turns out to be a short talk that I give, already late at night, to those attending.

It is worth commenting on this, on what I said. I look at the film, although not great, as a sort of benchmark film. Michael had said he had *Tristram Shandy* in his head when making this project; certainly the film about Manchester—Madchester—in the late Seventies and Eighties when the city took a lead first on punk music, then raves, through the likes of bands such as Joy Division and its reincarnation into New Order after the suicide of Ian Curtis, and the story of entrepreneur and mad ingenue Tony Wilson and Factory Records, are the story of a time and place when being young still was revolutionary. But given that the film was made after 'Welcome to Sarajevo', in 2001 coming out in 2002, given Michael's earlier work on Roddy Doyle's drama 'Family' in Ireland—I remember visiting that set--I argue that the film is indeed a political film—that with hindsight the 2001 date of its production is important, because it looks with fondness at the chaotic punk/rave period, at Manchester, while all the world is changing from the events of 2001. I argue that all that would follow— the movement towards conservatism, to control, to the politics of now and the wars of the Twenty-first Century, illustrate that demarcation. In a way, the film is not about the Seventies and Eighties, but about the love of chaos against the change the world experienced in 2001— and all that comes thereafter.

I also suggested, if I were teaching all, I would ask them to write an essay comparing 'Apocalypse Now', 'Party People' and 'Barbie'-- all as films that explore radical changes in society. And to this I add a reading of a poem from Yeats: 'The Second Coming' for good measure. That got everyone shaking their heads: the sort of reaction I like. Indeed crave. I can be the maddest of film teachers.

So I do not know what they made of me, but I enjoyed it. And I know I did indeed connect with some. As I told them: they too as young writers are on a cusp…a cusp of societal change, a cusp when their voices, their words, really matter. And I truthfully said I bow before them: I had seen how their talent and voices would reflect that world—and how they seek to change it.

*

Now: the next morning, and departures.

I am not one for goodbyes, especially to those who have come to mean more than a passing hello, a passing farewell. I rather sneak away; that is my way, and always has been. But before I do, I leave books for each of the young people as a gift. I thought Irish writers seemed appropriate, so four books each of Yeats' poetry for the poets of the group, four copies of 'Portrait of the Artist as a Young Man', four copies of Beckett's 'Waiting For Godot' and four copies of Claire Keegan's 'Small Things Like These'. All these works have a common thread for me: in each, words, sentences, phrases are carefully chosen. Words are chosen at random but rather hold weight, hold significance. Hold meaning. These works give voice to a truth that words really matter. This is the gift I leave for these writers, whose words touched me, and whose words in the future may guide me, may teach me on my own odyssey, as indeed as I hope perhaps I passed something to them.

Words, regardless of our language, give us Voice. And give us humanity…

*

Over the couple days in Ivano-Frankivsk I heard much, learned much. Stories, events tend to meld one into another and it is difficult to remember what happened when. But some of the stories I heard touched me, and I sensed that my presence, gratefully received, touched some of these young writers who I now follow and follow me on Facebook or other social media.

Amongst those, a couple I need to remember, to write down:

A young woman who looked to me about twenty, and I am not sure she was one of the 'students' there that year, came up to me to say how grateful she was that I had come, that it meant a lot. She also told me she had had difficulty coming to these events because her husband had been killed in the war, so seeing someone like me, reaching out, representing solidarity, meant so much….

I did not know how to respond to this. All I could do was tightly embrace her. She touched me deeply inside. I struggle greatly with a comment such as hers that is proffered not as a great revelation, but rather as a matter of course. Not a matter of fact, but part of one's journey and experience. One's pain. One's loss. It becomes my own.

And there was another young woman who came to thank me. She had studied law, as her father had been a lawyer. She explained that her father always told her that she should follow the rules, pay attention to the regulations. But then he hadn't. He had gone to war when Russia first invaded Crimea in 2014 and been killed. The authorities needed this girl (Iryna I think but now I cannot be certain) to identify the body, so she had had to go to the morgue to do so. Only the body could not be identified except by dental records….

One can only imagine. Or cannot. And again I am lost for words.

Experience does not teach about war. Not really. Only silence does. The silence of one's life.

There was the girl Iryna, another Iryna, who had studied at SOAS, who spoke beautifully in English as in Ukrainian, a fine writer who asked me to look at a book/pamphlet of hers written in Germany with a South Korean composer writing music and a photographer shooting his work, all together on an exchange/grant programme. I subsequently read her book; the essays she has written, the filmed performance of these artists working together, is fantastic.

It may have been the same girl, or another, it is hard now to remember, who had spent time in Montana—in Montana!—on a work exchange. She had had three options for work experience and felt Montana would be the most interesting—besides which she loved mountains. So she worked in a small town as a restaurant hostess. I can only imagine. A Ukrainian hostess in small town Montana…

There were the two young men I met, whose poetry touched me, and whose shyness compared to the girls I completely understood, because what might seem being aloof meant in fact something deeper—unsure how to connect, to talk, to be one and the same. They too I am in touch with on Facebook and Instagram.

And then there was the young woman who started to talk to me, and who ended up tearing slightly when realizing that I would be leaving that day.

It is not the tears that so moved me—it was an understanding that perhaps I had after all touched someone, someone who had helped me to understand about all of them, and who needed to know that an 'Other', someone from afar, really cares. Truly.

Their voices were, are magnificent. May they grow into the writers they are, and can be. They have touched me, and I carry them with me. Deep within a heart.

9-10 March
To Kyiv and arrivals

I am on the overnight train from Lviv to Kyiv. The train is Soviet era: long corridors, sleeper cabins for two in first class which I travel, functional space.

My cabin mate is the first grumpy person I have met. I ask if he speaks English: a little, but he clearly does not want to. I do not mind. Best to travel in darkness after some computer work. Best to travel in silence and get what sleep I can. Two sleeping pills do the trick: a few hours sleep after Ivano-Frankivsk and all the memories I carry now like clothes in the heaviest of steamer trunks—except that each piece of clothing within will be worn and worn again, without washing.

In the morning, a knock at the door. The woman attendant, out of central casting, has brought a cup of tea for me. I barely have time to knock it down, when we are in Kyiv.

Kyiv. As there are no functioning airports, the train station is the centre of the universe. And whilst it is only 0630, it is heaving—mostly with soldiers. Men and women. Young, and mostly young. I cannot help but wonder if I am the oldest person in the country.

It is too early to try to find my way to the hotel suggested by PEN Ukraine, so I sit in the 'concourse' nursing a weak cup of coffee I purchased at an open kiosk. Sitting, watching, unseen. Beside me a woman soldier; she does not look my way. I stare at the soldiers in their clean uniforms, marching up and down the corridor between the staircases leading down to trains to the east, and wonder. Will they survive? Will they fight. Will they live?

Will they die?

It troubles me. I was no doubt like they are in the staging posts of my day: the airports leading to a country half way across the world, a war I was too young to fight, too young to be forced to fight before it ended. But this war is different. This war is about survival.

An existential war, nothing less. What does that mean? That means to survive, to be, to live. Or to disappear forever.

None of these soldiers smiles. They are brave, but do not show bravura. There is simply a job they have to do; for them this really is an existential threat. So they will do their job. There is no room for doubt. No room for self-doubt. It simply has to be.

I remain there for a few hours, sipping at my coffee, staring at people. After a time most of the crowds of soldiers disappear, boarding their trains for the East, and the front. Boarding trains that might be called fate. Or luck. Or hope. Or destiny, I do not know. I think about it. I cannot join them: not exactly my fight, not exactly my war, and I fight in a different way. I wish much for each soldier, man and woman, that I see. Those that I do not. I wish that they live. Many will. Too many may not. One is too many.

I leave the train station and after some time figure out both where the incredibly deep Metro station is, and how things work. I trust google maps to lead me to the hotel. This time that trust works. I leave my bag at the hotel, to check in later, then return to the Metro. There is something I need to do. Something I always needed to do.

The Metro, followed by a rather odd old tram I jump on: I am not quite certain if I need to retouch my ticket on the reader or not (I do so regardless.) It does not take a huge amount of time for me to find the right stops. And from there, I walk some fifteen or twenty minutes.

Arriving at Babyn Yar is not a difficult journey, albeit a confusing one. But once there, things become muddled.

When I 'enter' into this wooded park, the first thing I am met with is the Soviet monument to the victims of Babyn Yar. The victims from Kyiv who died over the years of the war.

The years of the war, not the years of the Holocaust. The Soviets, the communist government of Ukraine, of Kyiv, distinguish between these two historical definitions. Jews are not mentioned. I know this from what I have read. The first monument is somewhat impressive. The bigger monument, ejaculating (a verb chosen purposefully) on a large, climbable mound, even moreso—as Soviet monuments go. Impressive but holding no emotional sway. These exist for statement. They do not exist for truth. Or memory.

And so I wander. I see some people out for a Sunday stroll, walking, pushing the odd baby carriage, chatting. To them this is simply a park. A place to walk on a Sunday. A morning out.

But that is not why I am here.

I wander further, slowly, this path and that. I look at the small ravines I see: was it here? Or was it here? I learn only later, towards the end of my few hours, that in fact it was largely everywhere.

Babyn Yar. In the US they say Babi Yar. I prefer the Ukrainian.

Babyn Yar. Here, in 1941, there was a huge ravine, canyonlike. You could put a car through it. Deep.

Deep as death.

Here, on 29-30 September, 1941, the Jewish population of Kyiv were transported to this ravine, told to strip naked and executed. Shot. The ravine then was one long ravine one hundred fifty meters in length, fifteen meters deep. The Jews of Kyiv were told to undress completely, were told to climb down, and then one on top of another Jew—shot. A simple statement to make. Killed.

Nothing here, however, is simple. The act was not simple.

In a ravine to be buried because they never were. Not to the Nazis. Not even sub- human. Rather non-human.

Except they were. Lived and, here, died.

Thirty-four thousand Jews.

Thirty-four thousand.

How do you shoot thirty-four thousand people here, I wondered. How does the mind allow it? How does the heart allow it? I wonder, staring at this abyss. Wonder. I still do. I do not have any answer. It is one of many questions.

And now, how do you indiscriminately send missiles and Shahed drones to a population to kill them? Kill civilians because they are. Or in the eyes of those who kill, simply are not.

Too many questions without answer. Explanations, but without moral answers.

So I wander further, deeper into this Sunday outing park, crossing a road, coming to the far side of this area. Here I finally find the memorial.

It was not erected until 1991, after the fall of the Soviet Union. They had prohibited a memorial before then. Prohibited remembrance. They too had attempted to erase Jews from history in their way of indifference and ignorance.

The story of Babyn Yar is told in many places, better than I can tell now. The details are known. What I see here, in this place of loss and death are two artists' installations, both fine work: one is a wall facing east in the direction of, and modelled after, the Wall of the Temple (the Wailing Wall) in Jerusalem; but from which in various places and heights along the wall juts out glass like shards. You are asked to stand with the shards along your side, your ankles, as if you are stabbed. It is interesting, in its way affecting.

Wailing wall. Wailing.

But perhaps affecting more for the head than the heart.

There is another installation. You walk down into an area that had once been flooded by the Soviets, to what is the central area of where the ravine would have been. Here is a huge polished steel platform, square. You can walk across, with tree-like aluminium or steel structures somewhat in the shapes of denuded trees reaching through the polished platform and upwards. No aluminium leaves grow here. These trees give no life. That is their purpose. Their statement. No respite. Look up, face God, close your eyes. Cease. You walk along amidst the trees, through them, alongside, up and down. On the shiny silver metal platform you walk across, in the tree-like metal structures too, are random holes, huge numbers of bullet holes, the same calibre as was used to murder Thirty-three Thousand, and more, Jews. As you walk, the name of every victim is read out on a speaker.

This memorial is more about the heart. The other the head. The intellect. But this, this is about loss. Never found. Simply and absolutely about loss. This I found deeply affecting. This asked me to remember, and in its way, to imagine. On this Gehenna, I can see, I can hear the cries, I can feel the tears.

Christ crucified. They know not what they do. Except they knew, and did.

Thirty-four thousand, one day.

Finally I walk back from this large pit area, this remnants of a ravine of death, up the hill, up Gehenna with memory as a cross, to where the Menorah, the primary memorial, about twelve or fourteen feet high, stands. Here I too, diminished, just a man, now stand quietly before this symbol that weeps and whispers, for a long time.

The voices of ghosts.

The harmonious voice of a woman, singing, mourning. Over a loudspeaker she sings with a fine rendition beautiful but sorrowful, Avinu Makeinu. I know the words in Hebrew from the years at Yom Kippur services as a boy in Denver. I know the song, now quietly sung here in Kyiv. It is one. It is the same. I know this is a part of me. I purposely lay three stones at the base of the menorah. A few others have as well, at some point in time. I stand there staring, considering for a long time. People pass here and there. Some glance, even stare, at me. One or two look at the Menorah, but interest is muted.

Memories do not last long.

Even the stories begin to disappear.

I do not. I will not. I cannot.

I stand, considering my own presence in this place, in this world. I have memory from within, that is a part of me. A part of what I am I guess. Now making its presence known. This too is a part of what I am.

A part of what I am.

Finally, finally I turn, walk away.

Avinu Malkeinu is a prayer of repentance. Or perhaps redemption: those two words are sisters to one another. They are joined as only siblings can be. Perhaps I am seeking both. And finding neither…

Thus I leave Babyn Yar. Or rather…I do not leave. Memory remains. I remain.

I too have become ghost. A ghost who whispers still.

11 March

I have arranged to meet Irish filmmaker and journalist Johnny O'Reilly, who lives in Kyiv. He had lived in Russia for a dozen years or so, setting up a company there, before moving to Ukraine. But as I am early, first I walk to Kyiv's St. Michael's Monastery, with its golden domes. As iconic as it is, overlooking the Dnipro River far below, the view over the city, magnificent, I am somewhat more taken by the 'exhibition' in the square in front: a shot up military vehicle that the retired soldier, wounded, so he tells me and shows me, was in Mariupol. Whether true or not, it gives pause for thought. The woven blue and orange bracelet I buy from him does as well. The showmanship of war, a purchase from small change. But for me, small change that triggers reflection. I know Mariupol. I have seen the images on screen. I have seen the death of that battle in story. The attempted Russian eradication of a city. That knowledge is pain. It rings loudly in my head, my heart, louder than any bells from St. Michael's might.

I then meet Johnny for lunch. We talk little of the war, more about filmmaking. He is working on a high budget feature documentary from the east, about the city of Kherson: its defenders. Its soldiers. Its survivors. He had been the sole westerner given access to a group of irregular soldiers whose work was assassination...or had been at first. Gradually they learned to trust him and agreed to go before camera.

However, as the Russian attacks increased, this unit's role changed. They were positioned to help people under fire, a role more about defence and helping those in need. The documentary in particular follows a number of separate stories. Later Johnny sends me a link to the work, which is extraordinary, strong and incredibly well made. He is now looking for equity finance while helped already by the head of the UK's Channel 4 Films, so there is not much I can add. He also sends me his written proposal and materials that he will submit for Eurimages/EU funding. I will offer suggestions then, but I cannot make the film itself any better than it is. In it, the voice behind already speaks. So I will make some funding enquiries but those I know are probably not able to assist; like everyone in this business not studio based, one scrounges for money. I think of enquiring through my brother into CAA, but know for both personal and professional reasons this is not an avenue really open to me. A pity. I do not do advocacy work, although this has the feel of it; any 'in' to CAA would be about entertainment. Johnny's work, his world, engages me, but is hardly entertainment. And coming on the heels of '20 Days In Mariupol' that has won its academy award, I can hear the refrain: but there is a film like this.

There is never a war, a missile, a shot, a death like this. The language of audience is not the language of each and every Ukrainian who does not submit. And who too often risks life for that language. Loses life for the words of that language.

I like Johnny. I think he is a very talented filmmaker. I wish there was more I could do. My direct access to equity funding is, alas, almost non-existent. My creative input might help, just slightly, on a funding application, but other than that I cannot be of much assistance.

*

After I leave Johnny I arrange to meet the poet Iya Kiva, not far from where I lunched. Naturally I get slightly lost as to the correct street and Metro entrance, as google maps points me in a different direction. In time we find one another and go for a coffee.

Iya is the poet for whom I had carried the train ticket picked up in Vienna, and who I met subsequently in Lviv. Here in Kyiv, in a café, we sit and chat. Sometimes I understand, sometimes I do not. But this much I know: she is a fine poet, a fine writer. I have read her work in translation. And she is truly a lovely person who has chosen too to bear witness, to take statements, to rail against an aggressor. She is someone I can listen to without always understanding. I hold her in highest regard.

After an hour I leave Iya. At home she has borscht to finish making (everywhere in Ukraine is borscht, but borscht as good as I have ever had—including my own.) I have then arranged to meet another documentary filmmaker, Nadia Parfin. I had traded facebook messages with Nadia. She had posted that she had been at a festival pitching—as I recall Berlin—but had found her audience inattentive and with no real understanding of her world. I had written to her that if there was any way I could help, or talk things through, I would be happy to meet—never having met her before.

On the way there, another air raid. Everyone ignores the sirens. So do I. These missiles or drones will not kill me, and if they do, so be it. I take the stairs into the Metro system. I stare at the children on the stairs. On the platform a lesson being taught to children who have left their classroom for the safety of the underground. Schoolroom with train. What will they remember, I wonder? The true lessons are there with them, not in the books or discussions, but there, in the chairs and makeshift classroom deep underground on this metro platform, with trains passing through. I remember feeling so pained that Covid had hurt children more than others. I feel the same now: their innocence has been stolen because of guided missiles and Iranian built Shahed drones almost daily launched into Ukraine, sometimes towards Kyiv. These are the lessons of the young. When to run. When to pray. How to study. How to remember. How to live.

And sometimes, how to mourn.

I manage to emerge from the wrong entrance in the Metro yet again, all too typically for me—and always confusing. I text Nadia and she tells me to wait. Again, commonplace. But she finds me. She is bright, and happy to meet. She takes me nearby to the 'Film House', a building once used by the Soviets and still retaining special union-like status that means its members can show whatever films they choose. There are a couple of bars in the building, a screening room, meeting places. It is like a Stalinist BAFTA of sorts, or Groucho's Club of the Soviet Era. I like it. They are immensely proud of it, as is the young owner of the building I am introduced to, who runs it and fights to keep it as it is. There are after all developers—and politicians who seek to develop—in every country.

We talk for a long time, about film, storytelling, art, words into images. Nadia wants to move into scripted drama. She is working on a short and asks if I will look at it. I am of course happy to do so and she will send it to me.

She talks of the actors and directors who work still, often out of this Film House. There is a screening on, a documentary, and an old time actor she knows is central in it. He will probably be there. She would like to stop in, so I join her. People seem to come and go during this screening, really just a stills photo documentary with voice over. Although hardly my taste in movie making, the fairly full room seems enraptured by what they are hearing. It occurs to me that any grasp at filmmaking, to a culture that once prided itself on cinema but now in which all monies have pretty much dried up, is to be held tightly, applauded, necessary even.

We are there for about twenty minutes, when Nadia leads me out. She has to leave but introduces me to friends of hers—an editor and his girlfriend. Both are friendly. The young editor is desperate to talk about his work. The girlfriend listens in part with apathy, in part because in truth it matters to her as well. We share glasses of cognac. I listen to the enthusiasm. I admire the youth before me, around me, the striving for potential to do wonderful things in film. I was like that once, before I became tainted by an indifferent industry dominated by marketing and ego. I understand the language. I understand the hope. Within I still quietly share it.

It is time to leave them and they lead me out of the building. They are good young people. I leave a card, but do not know if I will ever hear from them. Probably not. It does not matter. Sometime later, in touch with Johnny, I know he is looking for a Ukrainian based editor. I tell him about the young man I met, whose name I do not have. I put him in touch with Nadia Parfin. It turns out Johnny has worked with that young editor before, and will get in contact with him. Perhaps it will help, perhaps not. I am pleased to reach out, to make the attempt…

*

I have to stop back at the hotel to pick up some things, before meeting feature director Marysia Nikitiuk. I have been following and in touch with her, and trying to find a way to help Marysia, for almost two years now. I was first 'introduced' to her, or put on to her, by mutual friend, Spain based English film mentor Christian Routh, when war broke out in Ukraine. I had contacted Christian to say if there was anyone I could help, I would help. He in turn put me in contact with Marysia.

It is not of importance in what ways I have tried to help this dynamic, full of life young director over the past couple of years. Suffice it to say, she means something to me and I would have done whatever I could for her. She is a fine director, whose first film 'When The Trees Fall' speaks of raw energy and talent, of a director who has voice and is discovering ways to use that voice. Almost two years before meeting, Marysia had gone to Sarajevo, where I knew she was struggling: lonely, a bit confused perhaps. I had then arranged for some people I know—and one I barely knew because of the EUs Creative Europe, where I am a professional advisor—to keep an eye on her, to make sure she was safe. Ultimately she won a screenwriting award from Creative Europe/Sarajevo Film Festival for the project she has been developing, which I was terribly pleased to learn. The project, about both the Bosnian and Ukraine wars, and its effects on victims, is a story I well understand.

A year later I was in Sarajevo researching story material I needed for my own film project I was writing, 'In Memory I Will Find You'. I was pleased to have gone to Sarajevo, including a visit to Srebrenica that was difficult. And I understood, being there on my own and fairly isolated, what Marysia may have felt. It is a lovely city, but being isolated in a culture as I was then, and as I am in Ukraine, I understand and empathize with that loneliness, that sense of being at sea. This I share with Marysia.

Whilst in Sarajevo, perhaps eight months before this time now in Ukraine, I had arranged to meet a documentary director who Marysia described as her best friend, Alisa Kovalenko. Alisa is from the Donbas and had done a documentary that premiered in Sarajevo, a film about a group of young people who dream of a life beyond, and who are given the opportunity to go to Nepal trekking thanks to a Ukrainian radio personality. I had wanted to meet Alisa because I had wanted her to carry a copy of *A Requiem For Hania* to Marysia as a gift; Alisa had agreed to do so.

I had thought before I met Alisa that I should really try to see her feature documentary, which I was able to do at a late night screening. Watching that film at first I thought it very good, but lacking somewhat in narrative structure; the jump from Donbas to Nepal was not as clear-cut and understandable as I felt it should be. Always the film development story background in me looks at material critically, often too much so. A failing I have from too many years in the film business.

When I subsequently met with Alisa we talked about her film. I was complimenting it, rightly, when things began to hit me. I sat thinking that the teenagers in her film were like kids I knew everywhere—my kids, kids of my relatives, kids in Ireland, kids. Just…kids. Playful, bored, hopeful, hopeless, dreaming, scheming, trying to find ways to build relationships, losing relationships, to fall in and out of love, struggling with parents, wrestling with their own youth as they seek, and grow. Reflecting on this, quietly, sitting with Alisa as I was, talking, I became upset. I realized that I knew these kids without knowing them. I was touched by their stories. I had once been them. I knew them. And I knew that, at the end of the film when it said that some of the young girls had gone on to seek their dreams but the young boys had largely disappeared in the onslaught and chaos and indifference and loss of the war, I knew what this might mean for them all. And I recognized how lucky I was, how lucky were those I had grown or seen grow or cared about, who were able to lead lives and grow unhindered in this way. In many ways.

The lucky ones.

Perhaps this meeting, this reflection, was something that started me on the need to travel to Ukraine. Indeed looking back I think perhaps it was.

So now I was to meet Marysia, in person, at last, for the first time. And when I finally 'found her' waiting on the correct side of the cinema as we had arranged (I of course was on the wrong side), it was as if greeting an old friend, a dear friend. Perhaps a lost friend.

We embraced and whilst I do not think she would have quite understood, to me it was something special. She touches my heart as she had done so in the past, online, chatting, writing. Touches me too as she will do so in the future. She is a special person. I say this about a lot of people. Why Marysia is special, however, despite her unquestionable talent, is that she had found a way, from afar and without trying, to move me deeply. Because she is simply a beautiful girl trying to get by, to tell stories, to embrace life—at a time when doing so is frightening, and painful, and uncertain.

Marysia and I walk to a local restaurant. Although getting late we are able to have something to eat, and talk. After it starts to close, we go to a bar to drink some more, talk some more. Just talk. I listen to her, her stories, her projects, her fears, her love, her hate. Her dreams. I try to discuss ways I might be able to help, vague but desirous. Most of all I sit with her to let her talk, release. I sense her fears, her uncertainties. And her desire to have it all, to tell a story, to direct a movie again. To be known—not famous—but known as someone who has something to say and a means to say it. And like so much, and so many in Ukraine, she touches me deeply.

She mentions, and I need to mention here, one story that sets me thinking, hard. She had been asked and was helping—codirecting in part—her friend Alisa's documentary about the rape victims from the war in Ukraine. The same Alisa who I had met in Sarajevo a year earlier. They had been taking witness statements, were working on the film together. Now this struck a chord, as my film project 'In Memory I Will Find You' explores this subject fictionally during and after the war in Bosnia—and the progress of redemption from that conflict to today for three primary characters. So I listen to Marysia carefully, full of empathy. I know the stories, the scenarios. I have heard and researched and felt them for thirty years, since my first Bosnian screenplay written back in the mid-1990s, when journalist Janine di Giovanni helped me a bit with research.

The stories of rape, of hatred towards women, of inherent misogyny in a time of war, of the loss of identity and self, of sexual abuse, had been held within me as part of the awful stories from wars for a long time. I carry these as burdens of knowledge, part of why I feel I need to bear witness. Because the stories need to be told, and heard.

Thus I listen to Marysia quietly as she tells me about this project. However there is one shock that I had not quite grasped earlier. Her friend Alisa had been in the Ukrainian military for a time. I had known that. What I had not known is that Alisa, the quiet, smart director I had met, had been captured by the Russians, had been raped. She too was a victim, is a victim, now seeking to give voice to other victims who often do not have such a voice.

To tell the stories. To hear the stories.

I offer to help with this documentary in any way I can. To make contacts if it would be beneficial. But there are things I could not say, such as how much pain this subject causes in me, how much that pain hurts within. Things that are hard to say, particularly from a man.

I feel it all still. Too many victims.

As the night draws to a close, Marysia has consumed quite a bit of red wine, but insists on walking back to my hotel with me, about twenty minutes away. I am not sure if she has had too much red wine to drink because of the stories told, or because she is rather 'stuck' with me this evening, someone twice her age, or because of the nightly fear, the air raid fear, the fear of not being heard, the fear of death, the fear of not finding one's way. Perhaps all of these things.

When we get to the hotel, I insist on calling a taxi for her, although she keeps saying she can walk. My 'Bolt' account does not work for some reason but the hotel helps, and thus I put Marysia into a taxi to go home. I watch it disappear. I will see her again in Kyiv, but this night, necessary and painful, will be what will stay with me.

As will she.

12 March

This day's events are important to me. Along with the visit to Babyn Yar, this journey today is the one thing I had wanted to do in Kyiv. Thus I had specifically requested from PEN Ukraine if possible to assist with this journey—to see and understand what happened at Bucha. They were happy to oblige; it is a visit they often do with visiting PEN groups from other countries. I was a visiting group of one, representative of PEN Ireland.

At 9:00 the PEN Ukraine Mercedes van/bus arrives at the hotel. Two wonderful people will help guide me on a tour the Kyiv Oblast, to where the Russian troops advanced in February/March 2022, where Ukraine was able to repel that advance, and thus survive. But only just.

Many individuals, many fleeing, many defending, did not.

Many lives were lost.

In the van are Maksym Sytnikov, one of the PEN Ukraine young officers and their most trusted driver (who on many occasions would manage to scare the 'bejaysus' out of me on back-Ukrainian roads as he raced over them,) and Anna Vovchenko, a poet and also employee/member of PEN Ukraine. Anna is the more serious of the two, sometimes quiet. I learn she is also Jewish. She asks me for explanation when I say that I had purposely stayed with a Palestinian friend and her husband in Germany on my way to Ukraine. Anna struggles to understand this in the light of events, even as I explain that I have friends on both sides of this conflict, that I feel strongly that Palestinians and Hamas were not one and the same, that the wave of antisemitism I had been experiencing in Ireland and the UK were so appalling to me that the best way to counter such was to stay true to my beliefs, my personal ethics, and to those who are friends, whatever their opinion and their position on this conflict, as long as such I felt was just. And honest. And had nuance, which had so often disappeared from discourse.

Sadly this has not always been the case. I have lost friends because of this awful war in Gaza, not because of their political view on events there, but because their words and deeds bordered on if not sheltered antisemitism. Much of this has been incredibly painful, and in that I am not alone. It has also left me very isolated in Ireland, where antisemitism and its denial of such, its failure to recognize hurt, abounds. Perhaps this is one of the reasons I have so needed to come to Ukraine, without recognizing it at the time.

We subsequently drive out of Kyiv, through the suburbs, heading towards the district areas well outside the city, albeit only some forty to sixty minutes beyond the city itself. This is not quite suburb, but nor are these places 'somewhere else'; they are here, not there. Here.

Much of what occurred in this area is well documented, and does not bear repeating in terms of much of the historical context. The events in Bucha, in neighbouring towns, have been reported on, discussed, documented by the international press corps. Those events made the nightly news. They entered into the conversation. Nevertheless this visit now, bearing witness yet again, is an imperative.

Our first stop is the destroyed bridge between the city of Kyiv, and the cross over towards the small town of Irpin, just beyond. The bridge crosses the Bucha River here, the last gasp hesitation before moving into Kyiv from the North. The Ukrainian forces had blown the bridge up in order to stop the Russian advance. It is difficult to imagine what would have happened had they not done so. The Russians had then planned to put pontoons over the bridge to cross over its narrow river banks, so the Ukrainians flooded the river, making such crossing impossible for the advancing Russian forces.

The bridge remains a tangled monument. A spider-like memory. It will remain so. It has to remain so. Next to it is the new bridge that Ukraine has built, so traffic can pass. But the original, with a van still standing nose first at the edge of the river water, like a lone white bird with a broken wing struggling to reach fish to feed, resting against tangled concrete and metal rubble, remains as a reminder, a warning, a monument for the many who died here trying to escape. Many did die as the Russians shelled this place. Many thousands too crossed. Kyiv people hurried here and left their cars with keys in the ignition so that those who could would, and did, manage to escape the onslaught. At the side of this glaring wound, still oozing memory, blood and pain and dirt, sits a small stone wall where people have left messages of memory.

This too will remain. Memory is what they have.

In this place the Russians fired mortars, their gunfire against those trying to escape. Civilians trying to escape. So many never had a chance. Yet ultimately thousands were able to flee to safety, despite mortars, despite bombs from the air. I believe the total escapes numbered some 40,000, if I remember. But many still did not make it. They came in cars, on bicycles, in wheelbarrows, on foot and struggled to cross over the river. Many, far too many, died.

The bridge is an image that sears into memory. It will not be the last.

From the bridge we drive to the town of Irpin, just beyond. Here too many were killed, in the hundreds, as they desperately tried to escape. As you drive up the road, there is a central open parking 'lot' or parking area where learner drivers once would get their first driving lessons: not quite a track, more of a roadside layby.

Now, piled up as a monument of memory, an object of modern art that speaks only of loss and pain, is the huge mound of burned out vans, cars, all sorts of vehicles in which people had tried, unsuccessfully, to escape the Russian onslaught. Cars piled on vans piled on trucks piled on…The Russians shot those trying to flee, then burned the vehicles with bodies inside to try to hide the crimes. In what had been the front windscreen of one car sits a child's teddybear as a memorial. Bullet holes are everywhere. Some graffiti as memory: sunflowers from the ashes. Some names. A graveyard of cars. A graveyard of metal as an act of remembrance. Cars that had littered the town, the surrounding roads, were brought here, this graveyard, that all may remember.

Here as elsewhere the whispers and tears of ghosts.

We walk all around the mountain of metal. I take some photographs, although photographs never reveal the feeling one experiences here, the feeling of murder and loss and great pain. Of death.

Maksym tells me a story of a friend, a young girl who had done her driving lessons on this parking lot. When the Russians came she jumped into the family car to drive her family to safety. She, they, survived. It was the first time she had ever driven a car without an instructor beside her.

We stare in silence at this monument. This art installation that is not art, that is loss. The wind whispers volumes: we were here. We died here, in these burned out twisted metal coffins filled with bullet holes. We were you. Remember that; we were simply you.

As we stare we realize we are in the way of a car in which an instructor is giving a driving lesson. Things carry on. But not normally. Now the hazard is not simply bad driving. Now the primary hazard in the middle of this tarmac is what happened to so many who did not make it, who ran, who died.

I am silent as I look, and imagine, and feel this loss.

*

From Irpin we next drive to Bucha. Bucha is in fact a well-to-do middle class enclave still. Some who want to move out of Kyiv move to Bucha. Much has been rebuilt since the Russians came. Destroyed. Tortured. Murdered. Here was the scene of a terrible massacre, shown on news media throughout the world. People escaping were shot in the street, their bodies left to rot. Old. Young. Men. Women. Civilians. All civilians.

Some executed. Some tortured. Some beheaded. Some…target practice. No more than that. The Russian soldiers had been told that

Ukrainians were not human, did not deserve to live. So they shot. Killed. With echoes for me of Babyn Yar, etched in my memory…

Bucha was liberated two years ago today, as I type this. But many things are not forgotten. Those lost. The destruction. The fear. Now on the surface this town seems normal. So much rebuilt. Much of the destruction now disappeared. Does it ever disappear? We will have a good Ukrainian lunch later in town, I am told, at a restaurant that opened shortly after the Russians retreated because the owner wanted to make a statement, regardless of the poor condition of the restaurant after they had pulled out. I do not want to think about that now. The stories from Bucha are heartbreaking. Those stories are not mine. Not as I type; not when we pass through.

We drive down that famous, often photographed road where many lay dying. I shoot a photograph from the van. It speaks only in silence. The boy pulled from his bicycle, then shot through the head. The young man whose mother had to bury him in her garden, trying to protect his remains from dogs. The burned out cars. We do not stop. I do not want to stop. Life down this street now seems normal. Any street, any city. Anywhere. Ordinary. It is not ordinary.

Here the execution of civilian prisoners of war, their hands tied behind their backs. Here nine children under 18 murdered. Here burned bodies and torture. Mutilations. Beheadings. Here the dead lie uneasy. Ghosts.

Ukraine has too many ghosts.

We go to what was the library, the cultural centre. Now half collapsed, destroyed, the girders in the middle of the building resting at odd angles supporting no one, nothing. Walls caved in. A ceiling hanging against the open air.

Rain on our heads. Tears.

We see the mortar holes in the concrete walkway, forever burning a scar into the land. We go around to the back, overlooking a football pitch. Here too you can see mortar burn marks scarring the pitch. These places were deliberately targeted. No accident of misfiring here. Civilian places of sport, of culture. Targets. We look at the collapsed skeletal structure. Death throes. We stare at the intent of death still ever present. Sometimes we stare at death itself.

The next town is Borodyanka. We gaze, unflinching gaze, at the still half destroyed apartment buildings. Rooms exposed. Kitchen furniture on upper floors for all to see. A refrigerator of sorts. An oven, its small door hanging open. Walls gone. Lives lost. In a small glassed hut beside a half destroyed building, protected now by an alarm system, a Banksy graffiti mural artwork: image of a young girl in a karate outfit throwing a big, gruff man over her shoulder. Triumph of spirit brought here by another foreigner. Not forgetting. I venture a smile. Banksy witnesses as well—and even here there are some who would like to steal an artist's concrete graffiti canvas that has value.

We go to another cultural centre, again its facade largely destroyed. In the grounds in front, perhaps eighteen feet high, a statue of the 'poet of Ukraine' who means so much in this country of poets past and present, Taras Shevchenko. My guides want me to take note of the high velocity bullet hole through the statue's head. All indeed should remember, I remark: the Russians, I say, fear words, poetry, language, identity more than anything. Theirs is a statement of hate. The Ukrainians a statement of resistance, survival. The statue will never be replaced. Nor should it.

Fear me, for I am the word. And the word is the most powerful weapon.

Across the way, we stare at a shattered apartment high rise. On either side of it is empty ground. But once, two years earlier, there was a building on each of the wings of the one still standing. Those two buildings were destroyed by a barrage of missile fire. That was the Russian gift. Death in people's homes. I hear the words muttered: I have become death.

Death on empty ground.

We return to Bucha, seek out the restaurant for that promised lunch. And we also try, unsuccessfully as the gate is locked, to visit the Church of Andrew the Apostle, its grounds used as a mass grave because the mortuary could not handle the dozens of bodies, the dozens of murdered townspeople. The bodies have now been exhumed, receiving a proper burial. War dead and war crimes. A monument of names remains. Names not to be forgotten, as ordinary people are not forgotten. But their laughter, their greetings, their songs, their spoken dreams, their tears, their lives, these have gone silent. Even the ghosts here are silent.

That evening we drive back to Kyiv in silence. I am dropped off at the hotel. I change, then make my way to PEN Ukraine space for a poetry reading by my new friend, Ira Kiva. I sit in the back of rows, listening quietly, intently, reflecting on what I saw that day.

I do not understand the words. I understand the music. On this day I bore witness to the music, to the song. And although I did not understand the words, the music touched me. It remains with me. As it will through my days.

Iya later sends me a message about my having attended and listened to her poems, to the discussion that followed: "One of our topics was a language of body as a before-Babylon language and if we can understand each other without a natural language. Your presence was like illustration. I hope your next days in Kyiv will be fruitful for you. And I was really happy to meet you. IK"

Yes.

13 March

Much of the day is spent packing—not clothes, but books.

I travel with the PEN van, Maksym driving, to a warehouse somewhere along the river, and beyond, the Dnipro River that splits Kyiv in two. Anna has joined us. When we finally arrive, there are others I have met: the lovely Alyssa, PEN Ukraine exec who organized Ivano-Frankivsk; a couple young people I do not know but had seen at the reading the night before; eventually a French writer who I come to like quite a bit, Laurent Champs-Massart. Laurent and his wife Anne, who I am unable to meet as she has a writing deadline to finish, are world travellers who had come to Kyiv, and who had decided to remain. To help as and when they can. To write of their experiences. They write travel pieces, blogs, articles. Laurent has some experience in the book sorting business--certainly more than I have. They ran a bookstore in Bangkok once; who knew?…

We spend several hours putting mixed genre books, all in English, in boxes that will be distributed to various libraries throughout Ukraine. The books are all donated from the organization Book Aid International out of the UK. The generosity of this organisation is astounding. A true gift. So many libraries have been destroyed, that this is a way not simply of restocking, but of education, of voice-- indeed of hope.

We lunch on pizza, pack more, open boxes, close boxes, designate where they will go, and basically sort through hundreds and hundreds and hundreds of books. It is not particularly tiring or hard work, but it is good to do something relatively mindless. Quietly. Time to consider the images that have inundated for days. Weeks.

When we finally finish, Laurent helps me jump on a local bus—not like the buses I am used to, but half van half bus ferrying people around the city. He lives close to my hotel. We chat as he watches the city go by, again through the heart of Kyiv, until it is time to jump off. I recognize where I am and choose to get out at the same time. I do manage to get lost in the process, but eventually find my way back to the hotel for a spell.

That night I am on my own. I find a local Ukrainian restaurant for dinner in the centre of Kyiv. I wonder if I appear to those on the outside as I feel: a loner. An outsider. Un étranger. I probably do, but no matter. It is the path I have chosen.

14 March

I do find time to try to visit the Museum of Modern Art, or Gallery, or some such. I am always interested in what modern artists are working on; more so in a war zone. I take the metro and follow google maps, but cannot find the building. I find an office building and it would seem to be somewhere within, but where is rather beyond me. In walking to this place that hides what I am looking for, hidden not found, I pass some sort of urban military base. Soldiers all around. A target. I ignore it and am ignored. Everyone seems young. I would like to talk to these young men and women, but have no voice, no language. I admire them. I fear for them.

In the afternoon I meet with Marysia again for coffee, to chat. Coffee at her favourite cinema. I do like Marysia. I can see here in Ukraine she struggles, with production monies having disappeared, with dreams of telling stories in pictures stymied by a lack of possibility. We talk about her Bosnian project, about doing the next draft. We talk about her trying to get monies to attend a workshop/reading with story editors in Majorca later in the year. She will try to go but only if they can offer some sort of stipend to pay her way.

Money is that tight. We talk about a future. There will be a future but sometimes it is hard to see when you are young and in the midst of making a go of things. In the midst of a war.

I will do what I can for Marysia. Because I am so far out of the business now, it is not as simple as it once was. I will make some agent enquiries for her if possible. I believe she should be represented by an agent outside, in the US or the UK, to spread her wings more. To work on projects that can benefit from her voice, her talent, but are not constrained by who she is, where she is. I want to try to make it happen.

She sends me online links to her first film, 'When The Trees Fall', and her second, 'I Nina' aka 'Lucky Girl' so I can pass them on; and indeed in the case of her second film, so I might view it. I do weeks later. Although the film is in Ukrainian, shot in Germany, I can see Marysia's eye in the direction, her talent, her raw spirit, with an acting lead who is extraordinarily dynamic. The material is not necessarily remarkably original, but Marysia directs with aplomb and assuredness. I do hope I find a way to help her in the wider world. She deserves it.

That night I attend another reading at PEN Ukraine. The reading is for the fallen writer, Andrii Hudyma, whose first book, *69 Spices For The Heart* has recently been posthumously published. Andrii had been a chef, a bon vivant, a world traveller, a wonderful father to a young girl, Yulia. Clearly he was a larger than life character. The readings from his book start with a young woman who I immediately know must be that daughter, Yulia, after a short film about him. She had told people in the audience that they were to smile with joy at his humour, his warmth, his truly wonderful writings, but nevertheless there were tears. She read from the chapter titled 'Rosemary.' I do not know Yulia, but I can tell from her reading that this is a very special young woman. I love her spirit. I love what she is, and what she must have meant to her father. In a different world I would adopt her, or she more likely would adopt me. Andrii must have been so proud of her.

Even as she reads, I can smell the fragrant rosemary of the chapter that speaks volumes of herbs and spice and the warmth within…sixty-nine spices to warm the soul.

I realize from all around what this writer meant, what a loss so many feel, even as again I hear the music without hearing the words of the song. And I too find myself tearing at a loss of someone I did not know. And yet knew well.

As soon as the several readings are done, the discussion ending, I quietly make my departure. I would buy Andrii's book on display although in Ukrainian, but I feel my presence is perhaps out of place here, certainly not important. I should not be here I feel, not at this moment. It is not for me. This instead is a time for those gathered in collective grief and support and celebration, not for one who sat, and indeed sits, as an outsider. As an Other. But this much I do know: as this gifted man Andrii clearly found soothing humour, heat, warmth and indeed life in sixty-nine spices in the heart, in memory, in the complex and warming aromas of life itself, so too do I, as someone who loves to cook and who cooks well, know what he was about. In the sixty-nine spices and herbs of his life, my own touches his. The elements of a fine meal, and a fine life: life enhanced with possibility and aroma—and hope.

I wish I had known him. I wish I had dined at his restaurant, or sailed with him on his beloved sailing adventures, or embraced his daughter for her strength and courage. I wish I had known. In many ways, I had.

15 March

The way out—measured not in kilometres, or miles, or the time spent in a passenger van, but in the search one has to make to find oneself.

I am picked up at the hotel around nine in the morning. In the van are secure-hands driver Maksym and Tetyana Teren, deputy director of PEN Ukraine, whose kindness knows no bounds.

We drive through Kyiv and away, heading out to the suburbs and a somewhat distant metro station where we will collect the other travellers for these few days heading into the Chernihiv Oblast--the Chernihiv district.

I have no idea what to expect, who or what I will find. In the back of the van, loaded to the gills, are many of the boxes of books we had packed two days earlier. Part of the reason for the journey is to distribute these in the oblast.

Besides Maksym and Tetyana, I soon find myself accompanied by a distinguished group: the writer Sofia Andrukhovych, whose latest novel *Amadoka* is a sensation in Ukraine and is being translated into English by Simon & Schuster; the academic and often my own translator, Sasha Dovzyhk, who taught at Birkbeck and is setting up an institute in Lviv (I was supposed to meet her in Lviv, but all wires got crossed)—who I instantly find approachable and warm; the broadcaster Myroslava Barchuk, a celebrity journalist and filmmaker who has turned to podcasts because of Ukrainian broadcast politics, or so I gather, brilliant in her way; the writer Kateryna Kalytko, poet, historical writer—thoughtful, quiet, very bright; and finally the philosopher, teacher and lover of Spain and Irish whiskey (or will be with me thanks to St. Patrick's day a couple days hence) Vakhtang Kebuladze, whose great intellect is immediately apparent, and who I think perhaps does not know what to make of me at first. He is good for a smile, for thought, for discourse with all (when he picks out a book of Jack Kerouac's to talk about to a group in a library, I know I am in decent enough company.) Bidding us farewell at the Metro station is the head of PEN Ukraine, Volodymyr Yermolenko, a philosopher and brilliant mind. I had first met him in Ivano Frankivsk, although I had seen him in discussion online with Philippe Sands months earlier; I already know that as an intellect his is equal to any. Like some of the others, he looks at me with a wary eye, but I sense nevertheless he appreciates that I have come along, albeit for the ride.

I will not write portraits of each of my companions here; to do so would require volumes. I will leave it that I was and am in awe of each of these talents, voices, writers, human beings. Each one of them is special, brilliant in her/his own way, committed and honest. I can only say that they will be forever etched in my memory and mind as good people who allowed me a glimpse of their world, their words and their kindness to me, an 'Other', an étranger—in all of Camus' meaning.

With all of us finding seats in the PEN minibus van, replete with coffee and necessary morning buns after we quickly stop at a petrol station, we begin our journey from the outskirts of Kyiv north to the Chernihiv Oblast. Chernihiv sits on the border with Russia and Belarus. When the Russians started full scale war in February, 2022, Chernihiv stood just in front on the road to Kyiv.

The Russians occupied Chernihiv more or less for forty days. Chernihiv City, with its Unesco designated centre of international importance for its monastery and churches, was put under siege, although held with minimal damage by the Ukrainian army. The outskirts of the city were 70% destroyed. Towns, villages in the oblast were occupied. As the populations of the district did not emerge to welcome the Russians as liberators, they were thus enemies. Those who the Russians felt had no right to exist. Who as easily could die as live, without care. Certainly without mercy. Thus many were killed. Many became refugees in their own country and well beyond. Many places were destroyed. The Russian way. Forty days of the worst oppression, execution, fear.

We were now ferrying boxes of books to a number of libraries in the district that we would deliver over three days. Books mean not simply stories, but history, culture, hope, art, language—and freedom. Libraries, as in the places I had seen in Kyiv Oblast, mean hope. The Russians sought to destroy hope, to destroy identity.

They could not succeed. They did not succeed.

I have long said that words matter, that words are our weapons. In Ukraine there is truth in this. Words—books, poetry, culture--are a means of fighting back for those who do not carry guns. And for many who do, as I have read in the poetry published and from recitals coming from the front.

So these books are our weapons.

One of our first stops on this day, however, was not at a library with an awaiting audience and committee eager to greet us.

Instead, we drive to a hamlet more than a village, a place called Yahidne. Here, seven days after the invasion began, the Russians entered this small place, pulled the residents out of their homes, and forced them into the damp, dark cellar of a small local school that the Russians had made into their headquarters—and by doing so, had human shields in the local population.

We are met at this delapidated building by Ivan, caretaker and grandfather who had been kept in the cellar, along with his son and two grandchildren and the rest of the townspeople: some three hundred fifty people, for twenty-seven days. His eyes are red not from lack of nightly sleep but instead reveal a tiredness, a weariness, that goes far beyond. His quiet voice, his pain, his witnessing and need to tell a story are like nothing I have ever quite encountered. He does not shirk away from what happened in this place. He does glorify survival.

He tells a story, and the pain of that story, because all need to hear, and see, and in our case now, feel and touch. Mostly feel.

And whilst I cannot understand that story except in translation, I too see, and feel, and am moved. And am pained.

Ivan gives us a long tour of this cellar, with its several rooms. In the largest, the size of perhaps eight ping pong tables, one hundred fifty people had been kept within. On the door frame of each room there are numbers to say how many people were in each, so the Russians could keep track of those living—and those who would not live. The rooms were so cramped that people could only squat on the floor. Body sores became commonplace. Old people, parents, young people. No light, damp, stifling air, no toilets. No privacy for the buckets and potties that were used. Children were kept here. Babies. Many people died. For days their bodies remained with the living until the Russians would allow a few to be carried to the kindergarten shed above. Ivan tells a story of one woman whose infant struggled to breathe in the damp. The Russians would not allow her take the baby upstairs for fresh air. What did she expect, they asked? This is war.

This is the face of their war.

And torture.

On the walls, graffiti. Drawings by children. A drawn football pitch for a match that would exist only in noughts and crosses. Days being marked to keep track, expecting the final day to mean death— as the Russians promised.

In the large room, a couple torn, beaten sofas. A couple chairs. Potties. This is all they had. Here and there scattered rags, clothes, a couple toys. The room damp. The air fetid. Death not life. The fear of dying. The fear of extermination. Of disappearing. Each item in the room remains marked as a memorial. As evidence. For people like us to bear witness. Perhaps for war crimes investigators. Everything is marked, numbered—marked perhaps as the scene of a crime, marked too so that no one forgets. Whomever visits now, no one forgets.

We quietly go through each room. Each life that was here.

One day the Russians ordered men to go upstairs, to the open air, to dig a trench. The men were certain they would be shot and buried in a mass grave.

They weren't. They could have been.

During the day the Russians occasionally, rarely but occasionally, allowed people outside to use the toilet in what had been a kindergarten building. At night, however, there were those three buckets for one hundred fifty people. And the few children's potties.

Once they brought a loaf of bread for the villagers. Mouldy, it was at least something fresh. Some mothers hurried for a piece to give their children. Sometimes there were crackers offered. Often times—not.

Once they brought some food that diesel had been poured over.

Everyone was hungry.

An old woman was the first to die. Her body could not be removed.

No electricity. At night only darkness and fear.

On the wall etchings of the dead. The old. A child. It took days to get permission to bury them.

Chicken pox. Swollen legs from lack of movement. Breathing difficulties. Things happened too difficult to say. To write.

Ivan's red eyes.

My silence.

A few questions asked. The need to know. The need to understand. Again to bear witness. My philosopher friend Vakhtang needs to set up a podcast. My friend Sofia keeps notes in her head for an article she needs to write. And I, I stare. This is not because I am a war junky, or because it is an adrenalin rush, a bit of a Disneyland for the future visitors as I once saw and felt when touring Auschwitz. This is raw memory. Because stories need to be told.

And Ivan needs to be heard. He was here, and he wants no one to forget. He owes it to those who survived. And those who did not.

This was the face of war. Of innocents. Of victims. Of the dead and those who did not die and then who would go on, yet remained dead inside. And will. This is what torture means to those who simply existed in a place, at a time, in war.

It was hard not to stare at this place. To think we are the lucky ones. Not to shed tears. Gaping at this place of pain and death. And yet that is part of the job. My job. Bearing witness is painful. And necessary. The story must be told and retold. We must tell it. So that it will not happen again? It will. But these people, these victims, deserve their story should be witnessed, and spoken, and remembered. It is not who they are. It is what happened. It is them.

And it is heartbreaking. Beyond words.

*

One of our first library visits is in the town of Mena. Mena itself is bustling. The library is rebuilding. It had survived the occupation without much damage. We hear stories of what happened in this small, pretty town.

Mena is surrounded by waterways, so many people came here seeking safety as it was a larger place. Safe it would not be. Not during the occupation.

The librarian tells us a story of a woman who arrived on a boat with infant twins at her breasts. All the bridges were down so Mena was the only place she and others could go despite the risks. When she stepped off the boat she would not let go of her twin babies. She would not let go, wanted never to let go. I wonder if she will ever learn to do so.

The librarian tells of how the people in the town heard the constant stream of fighter jets flying low overhead. They knew the jets flew to drop bombs on Chernihiv City, their beautiful Chernihiv, but there was nothing they could do. They were under occupation for forty-three days. One Hundred Sixty tanks passed through the town. Nothing they could do.

The area, particularly the library, is rich in community spirit. The food they made for us wonderful. The local townspeople who met us, listened to an introduction of books, gratefully received, are gracious people. The area is known for its local drink made in stills on farms, a sort of Ukrainian poitín. The librarian tells a story: because the farmers often had yeast, they gave it and flour to every nearby village so they could make bread again, once the Russians had withdrawn. They sent it down to Yahidne; they heard what had happened there. They share recipes, food and faith. Their spirit to survive, to survive as a community, is ever present.

<u>15-17 March</u>
The Libraries

In the mornings we meet at breakfast in the hotel located in the centre of Chernihiv. I mention this in passing because each of the mornings there I note the American and English voices at a table beside mine. Two or three bulky men. I wanted to engage with them but don't; they do not seem interested in our group despite my American English accent. To me it is clear they are, or were, military. Discussing it later with my companions, whilst these men may have been staying/based in Chernihiv to help address reconstruction issues, given their look and demeanour it is very possible if not likely they are sappers, or working with sappers.

The Russians left IEDs everywhere outside villages and towns, and it will take years to clear these—if possible, as long as possible. Thousands of mines. The next tragedy Ukraine will need to address. Knowing what we know about Iraq, Afghanistan…we know what might happen.

Ukraine is now the most mined country in the world. I am warned that I must not wander off wherever we are; stay with the group. Most mine fields have yet to be identified. Hard to identify when missiles and drone attacks continue. And they continue every day. Sometimes it is difficult to remember this is a war zone. But the images of war remain, if not on the surface, just below.

I am reminded once again of Wisława Szymborska's poem 'The End and the Beginning':

> After every war
> someone has to clean up.
> Things won't
> straighten themselves up, after all.
> Someone has to push the rubble
> to the side of the road,
> so the corpse-filled wagons
> can pass.
>
> Someone has to get mired
> in scum and ashes,
> sofa springs,
> splintered glass,
> and bloody rags.
>
> Someone has to drag in a girder
> to prop up a wall,
> Someone has to glaze a window,
> rehang a door.

>   Photogenic it's not,
>   and takes years.
>   All the cameras have left
>   for another war.
>
>   We'll need the bridges back,
>   and new railway stations.
>   Sleeves will go ragged
>   from rolling them up.
>
>   Someone, broom in hand,
>   still recalls the way it was.
>   Someone else listens
>   and nods with unsevered head.
>   But already there are those nearby
>   starting to mill about
>   who will find it dull.
>
>   From out of the bushes
>   sometimes someone still unearths
>   rusted-out arguments
>   and carries them to the garbage pile.
>
>   Those who knew
>   what was going on here
>   must make way for
>   those who know little.
>   And less than little.
>   And finally as little as nothing.
>
>   In the grass that has overgrown
>   causes and effects,
>   someone must be stretched out
>   blade of grass in his mouth
>   gazing at the clouds.

I think of this poem often during my travels. It is a sort of keystone poem for me, a warning perhaps, not heeded. I referenced the poem in *A Requiem For Hania.* I remembered it in Lviv. I find I am drawn to it time and time again these days. Although written about the Second World War and the Holocaust, nothing has really changed since then.

Nothing really does.

*

Over the next three days we visit libraries in towns throughout Chernihiv, towns with names like Mena, Grodno, Novgorod-Siversky, Bobrovica.

In some of these towns libraries had been rebuilt or refurbished after the Russians left, with many people held captive for forty days.

Some libraries were untouched. Others were completely destroyed. Knowledge is power. Words are weapons. The Russians sought to destroy these weapons, these words, this identity.

In some of the libraries we find modern rooms and wonderful collections. Others are just beginning to rebuild their stacks, their collections. Their lives.

Some stories are worth repeating here, even if the towns in which these stories emanated become confused by a language I do not know and a rushed weekend.

Everywhere we travel, we are met with much food laid out for us as a welcoming gift. In the first town the local villagers were a bit disappointed we are late, because their local specialty dumplings had grown cold. Cold or not the different foods on display for us are not simply delicious, their gift touches me in ways hard to describe. The academic Sasha, who became my good friend, reflected later: *"for these people, memories are long. During the Stalin years, a famine had been created by Stalin's agriculture and collective policies. For them to offer us this food, not long after occupation, is more than a simple offering. Often these people have little, but the gift we are bringing them means much, and their gift of homemade foods in return means sacrifice. Never forget how much was sacrificed."*

In another town, I think Mena, a documentary produced by Myroslava and with commentary by some travelling with me now, the second in a series, is shown in the modern library. It is a film about the history of Russian imperialism in Ukraine, about the war now and the Russian view that Ukrainians have no identity—and thus their victimization is meaningless to Putin and his followers. It is a film too about the arrival and rebirth of modern Ukraine. Myroslava had hoped the film would be subtitled for me, but it was not to be. As I sat watching regardless, the librarian appeared and drew me alone out of the room, knowing I could not understand the film.

She took me downstairs, where to my amazement two young musicians had been playing British and Irish songs for a small audience, as the following day was St. Patrick's Day. A guitarist and a woman with a tin whistle. The audience had broken up, but they wanted to play a song just for me, their new Irish friend. The Irish reel was a wonder to be heard, there in the far north of Ukraine, just a few miles from the Russian border. A place that only two years earlier had been under occupation by the Russian army, where such display would have never taken place. This music, fantastically performed, touched me deeply. There is a wonderful photograph sent to me later of my arms over the shoulders of this lovely couple. The woman who played the tin whistle had once been to Ireland. The young guitarist had not. But they loved the music and the sounds of the country I now call home. And they loved that I, someone from Ireland, had come to see them, to hear their music. That I was, simply, there.

The music heard, even if I could not understand the words....

At all the libraries everyone wanted photos taken. A couple of young girls were keen to have their photos with each of us, to show we had visited, that they mattered in a world so far from their own. They are lovely young women who become friends on Facebook, on Instagram. What they see in befriending an old person such as myself is a bit beyond me. Or perhaps it isn't. It is not the modern equivalent of pen pals. Instead it is an acknowledgement not by them but my me that they are, they exist, they live and breathe and laugh and take selfie photographs of themselves and their world as do all young girls everywhere. That is the lesson they hope--no, need--to disseminate. To be known, remembered. Just like anyone's daughter, sister. Just-- girls. And that is a statement in itself, given what happened here, what is happening here still.

And every so often, now here, back in Ireland, when I post a photograph of my landscape, my dog, my world so far away, yet not so far away from their own, they are the first to respond: because they want me to remember them. Their lives, like mine, despite the gulf of distance, of age, are so much the same.

And even today, as I review these words, editing, correcting, I know that only a few hours ago missiles fired by Russian struck

Chernihiv. Struck their world. May they be safe. May they only be safe...

At another library, another young woman—because it is mostly young women since the young men are away, fighting, sometimes dying; I need to remind myself always of this--is keen to show off her English speaking abilities. She teaches young children, as I recall. Or is perhaps an assistant librarian. She tells me I should visit the museum nearby; I say I hope we get to.

In fact we do visit this museum: a museum to the iconic Ukrainian filmmaker, Oleksandr Dovzhenko, whose film 'Earth' is a Soviet era classic. And there is the rub. This had been his house, once. Dovzhenko was as important a filmmaker (then Russian) as Eisenstein. The small house/museum is amazing, with photos, awards, a history, posters, ceiling and walls adorned with amazing artifacts. In the courtyard a large statue of the director—one the Russians had not destroyed, in part because Dovzhneko is considered one of theirs. It leads to an interesting discussion about the nature of culture, and how the Russians sublimated Ukrainian culture to create an image of what culture should be. Dovzhneko is a hero, but one with question marks because of the Leninist, later Stalinist, regime he worked under. If nothing else, the museum is a fascinating diversion, where art and politics met and meet, where the war touches and does not touch. His silent film 'Earth', which I only watch back in Ireland, is at once a masterpiece of image but also a sounding board for Soviet collectivism propaganda at the time.

There lies the conflict between art and lies. And there lies the central cultural argument raging in Ukraine. Indeed I see the argument when foreign culturalists discuss, and are discussed. All too often those from my world might bring up Dostoevsky or Tolstoy as examples of 'Ukrainian' art that is not Ukrainian. I would prefer to talk of Babel, or maybe Gogol, both born in what is now Ukraine. But they too are the product of the Soviet world, and the Soviet nightmare. The Russian nightmare, past, present. For Ukrainians, history is long, but also short. And the dialogue needs to change, even if the arguments do not.

Then there is the library of Novgorod-Siversky, a fascinating, uncomfortable visit. We are met here and escorted to the basement. I later learn that this library, not far from the Russian border, is still hugely at risk. Everyone needs to be wary. Careful. The people, oddly, are the coldest, an odd assortment of older people without a young face in sight. Serious looks, not happy. Again one might say they are straight out of central casting.

At the head of the long table where we are asked to sit in this windowless room, is a man who could be a mafia hit man. He is a tough looking character, occasionally displaying a bitter irony, but never a smile. I watch him, thinking I know the type. He is in fact some sort of deputy head of the council. Sceptical about us, our purpose, our words, to put it mildly. But I think there is always an Achilles heel. Walking down the stairs into the basement, Tetyana had whispered to me: we will not be reading as normal; we will go with the flow. Clearly the reception we find has not been expected.

We sit in a panel at the table, and my fellow travellers begin to explain who they are, what they do. We are met with silent stares—not warm, but not overly threatening. It is hard to understand exactly what it going on, and why.

Sasha whispers to me that these people want me to speak as well, that she will translate. I sense the slight warning.

So I am introduced, and when I am asked to speak I am not quite sure what I am supposed to say. What I say, therefore, is that I have come here to understand, to witness. To show my support and kinship. To show they mean something not only to their fellow countrymen, to these wonderful writers, but to people like me in the West. To say they have not been forgotten. And in talking I somehow find the right words to reach out to them. I tell these people that it is the day before St. Patrick's Day, the most important holiday in Ireland. I tell them that for the Irish, St. Patrick's Day represents, freedom, independence, hope, possibility. The luck of the Irish. The dream of a future. I tell them that this is what I wish, and now see, and dream of, for Ukraine.

They nod their heads. They understand this message.

A man at the back stands to read a poem he has written, full of patriotism and bravura. He too is a poet. A poet of need. A poet of their dream.

The meeting is over. Tetyana later tells me that what I spoke was perfect; she clearly is pleased.

We are taken to a small room upstairs. Once again food has been laid out for us, some wonderful things. I purposely sit at the head of the table beside the councillor, this tough, alpha male. A fighter perhaps. A 'don'. He occasionally looks at me without a smile. But I know that I am the oldest present, that I can stand up to scepticism. So I alone agree to share a shot of vodka with him. And a second. And we touch glasses. Because I know--him, what he will have been through, who he is, who he wishes he could be. And I know that somewhere behind him too is a family that he just wanted to see survive, and grow, and be safe. Because I do understand, an understanding that comes with age, and distance, and weariness at all I have seen in this life. And not wanted to see.

Because I am a Jew who has borne witness. And survived to tell stories. That is the lesson…

It is then that I am reminded by Sasha that these people once had nothing. That this matters. And told later that partly why there was unfriendliness at first was that we were the first writers who had visited this town since 1989. 1989. Thirty-five years later. Thirty-five years late. All they had been offered, all they had known, all they had been told so close to this border, was Russian: writers, television, culture. These people felt forgotten. When the Russians of this war came through they could not be stopped. But they could be hated. And yet for this town, this place, they had yet to be included in this new identity, this need of their homeland so often taken away over these thirty-five years. Even still they had to hide in the cellar to greet people such as us. So thirty-five years later we show up. And say we are another way. Thirty-five years late.

And we are a different way, a direction for which they will still have to fight, and be patient, and mostly not be forgotten. Never again forgotten.

In my heart, I tell myself I will return here. Because I said I would, somehow, one day.

I hope I can. And share a shot of vodka, and a toast, with a hard man. For that is the truth: I am his Achilles heel, and I want him to know that I am here, and there. I really hope I can return…

*

There is one final story to mention in the visit to libraries over these days. The library in Grodno is a special place. Grodno we would say in the UK, in Ireland, is a market town, large, many of its houses displaying the familiar sky blue painting on their fronts, with window canopies and sideboards often lace like, old fashioned and beautiful. These facades are typical of Chernihiv and well on display in the town.

The library is located in the centre. It is well-to-do. The parking area looks out on shops that could be a market town in Ireland or the UK.

On this day, St. Patrick's Day, we each grab the final large cartons of books we will gift and begin to carry these inside, standing first on the steps for the obligatory group photograph. We are then met by the head librarian, an effervescent, energetic woman full of smiles and chat and boundless energy. She makes me laugh.

It seems however they had not quite expected us. This day is a local holiday of some sort and they are preparing for a local concert in the library auditorium. The women helpers, the librarian, all wear the local costume of the area, white dresses with beautiful patterned designs embroidered by hand.

The librarian begins to take us on a tour of this wonderful library, which clearly is a cultural hub for the town and far more than a library. The Russians had occupied the town for several weeks, but had left this building untouched—although a library on the outskirts was destroyed.

We visit many of the rooms in the building, a grand tour of which they are all very proud. In one there is a large trampoline for exercise. In an upstairs rooms small fitness trampolines for children and adults alike (and very small children, as I would see), replete with a blood pressure machine. Another room holds an auditorium. One room is the children's library with caged rabbits and hamsters just at its entrance. Upstairs, the language library with several desks relating to different languages: English, French, one or two others, with books, grammars, information on the languages and places. There are stacks of Ukrainian and foreign language books. A computer room. A classroom.

Clearly this place is a hub of a well-to-do community, very middle class, with its library at the centre of its cultural life. What intrigues me most is a large alcove space where local women gather to sew and darn and embroider, to work on craft. But it is what they are working on here that I find most extraordinary: they are making camouflage nets for the army, sewing them by hand. And nearby, on the walls, photographs of local boys: who they are, their names, their stories, where they have served. Where they have died.

Here in this wondrous place, more dynamic than many libraries I have seen in the UK and Ireland, even in the US, the war is not far away. It is in fact only thirty miles or so away. Quiet now, this front. It should always be so, but the likelihood is that it will not.

This is what a foreign imperialist country wants to take away.

And this, I know, is what other foreign countries dither about when asked to offering protection, defensive weapons. What those where I grew up cannot understand is that this place is no different than their own. That the people here simply want to stand tall, to say this is who we are.

And we are you…

We return to the ground floor, watch as the singers in the concert appear on the stage and the lights dim. Women in their native local costumes, echoing the lace on windows of houses, with headdresses, begin their song. We stay and watch for just few minutes, stopping at the table outside laden again with local delicacies, encouraged to try this cake, this dumpling. It is as if my grandmother was scolding me: eat, eat…Grandmothers everywhere, Jewish or not, are the same. And I need to remind myself that I am now of the age where I would be one of those grandparents. At least this time much will not go uneaten, as the food is for everyone who has come to the concert.

But now it is time to leave. The books have been put into a back storeroom—appreciated but not as unusual, or in need, as other libraries we have visited. This time we only get to chat with some of the librarians and helpers. And once again, unsurprisingly, there is a lovely young woman who is desperate to speak English; it has been a long long time since they had visitors. We are given a gift as we leave—a bag with a local tourist brochure. A fridge magnet that shows a painting of one of the young women of the area in costume

May they have tourists one day in the not distant future. Tourists who do not come in combat gear, 'tourists' who speak only Russian, and who seek to destroy this magical hub that breathes huge life into this town.

17 March

Afternoon, and a rush back to Chernihiv city from that last town, that final library. The roads here are mad—not with traffic: there is little. But the roads are pockmarked from time, and lack of care, and mostly from the tanks and transports that had come down this way two years earlier. Who can say if they will ever be repaired. Maksym understands these roads and drives somewhat like a formula one driver, always in the middle of the road, slowing at blown up bridges with ways around not always easy to see, only stopping for the many checkpoints or anti-tank placements and 'hedgehogs' requiring that we slow, show identification, nod.

At one such, near a sign, we stop to get out, to take a photo. The soldiers at the checkpoints some hundred meters behind—men and women soldiers—watch probably with some amusement. Wary perhaps, but the 'PEN' people carrier is the last of the threats they concern themselves with.

A picture taken but do not wander: we cannot know when there is a field of IEDs waiting to maim. Or kill.

We return to Chernihiv city after the visit to Grodno, noting on the outskirts of the district's main city the massive destruction the Russians had left behind, although much rebuilding has been accomplished. We stop at a petrol station for some things and with encouragement, and a promise that needs keeping, I buy a bottle of Jameson whiskey—for there are bottles to be had, and it is St. Patrick's Day. I had suggested that this was the way to celebrate the day. Encouraged by Vakhtang, I make good the promise and we all imbibe a little…I do try to keep up with Vakhtang, although I'm not the best at holding my liquor. But the occasion matters in Ireland. And now it matters—greatly—in the Chernihiv Oblast of Ukraine.

We are joined by a few others for a tour of the churches and monastery in the centre of Chernihiv, those churches designated as a likely Unesco site, somewhat worn down by the indifference of the previous regimes of Ukraine. And Russia. The guide, dressed in medieval garb with a wooden sword and dagger in his tunic, is no doubt amusing, although as is said to me later, it was a bit of a tour more for youngsters than the historians and philosophers with us. Regardless, as all information is in Ukrainian, my eyes wander and speak enough for my personal understanding.

The churches are undoubtedly beautiful, but as is explained in asides to me, much of their history is false, as the guide is eager to inform, created to give the Russian Orthodox view of history, their narrative, rather than the reality of the Ukrainian narrative. The stories are interesting, no doubt amusing at times, but I am not particularly engaged, and I am not convinced our group is as well. It is part anomaly, part juvenile history lesson, part underlying denial of the propaganda that was of the Stalinist/Russian Empire story, a story all now want to change. Especially the young guide. Truth, and history, matter now more than ever before. And must be released from the yoke of the Russian empire as never before.

We meet for lunch in a restaurant known for its fish, awaiting a concert that is intended for the afternoon. The concert includes a philharmonic youth orchestra and two apparently famous singers who we had met at breakfast and for reasons I understood later—because I was Irish and they had performed in Ireland—had taken a bit of an interested shine on me.

The concert is delayed: an air raid. People are not allowed into the theatre. But the air raid clears, and I am assured by all that I and Sasha Dovzyhk will make it back to Kyiv in time for us both to catch the night train to Lviv. I will be heading back on from there west back into Poland, and already finding that realisation difficult.

The concert, in honour of the national poet Taras Shevchenko, is fantastic. The music was composed to his poetry, and the two women, in pastel 'ferry' skirts, perform as if their lives depended on it, with the young concert orchestra. These are the Telynuk Sisters, Lesya and Halya. They are, it is explained, almost national heroines. My fellow travellers had grown up with their music and their singing; in patriotic fervour the songs and the poetry of Shevchenko seizes the moment, as do the wonderful musicians.

After the concert, we are invited to a back room. The requisite hospitality, food, drink, the lovely sisters and the conductor who I realize had been on the tour of the churches with us earlier. One of the sister's husband is her manager and promoter; it is his birthday, so 'Happy Birthday' in Ukrainian is sung. The organizer of the event, a lovely man who made a fortune I think in the water business, or perhaps it was mining of some sort, is an underwriter of many PEN events as well. He is a lover of Irish whiskey. Because we had come to celebrate, I had rather foolishly hidden the bottle of Jameson under my coat to carry in for the concert—I had been terrified of dropping it during the performance. But it, and I, survived; so I put the bottle on the table for any who wanted to drink. The organizer, however, looked at it rather with disdain, as he had brought a bottle of up market 'Crested Ten' Jameson and would not deign to drink from my inferior aged examples of Ireland's nectar. Still I raised the glass in my hand for a couple toasts, wishing all a Happy St. Patrick's Day. I am not certain that any copped on, ever, that my passport, although held for more than twenty years, whilst making me legitimate, did not necessarily make me a true Irishman. Still, there were moments when that masquerade, or half-truth, needed reinforcing.

The glasses of Jameson whiskey raised with smiles, for my sins, no doubt helped. As is said often in Ireland, slainte.

We finally break away from the festivities and hurry to the van. It is time to return to Kyiv. We leave the city largely in silence. I think Vakhtang is somewhat annoyed that I had left my bottle of whiskey back in the party room. But so it goes.

It is dusk, then night, as we drive back towards Kyiv. The lack of light is at times eerie. The silence adds to thought. As does the rain, which grows heavy as we head south.

We get another air raid warning on our phones as we leave Chernihiv. This one does not disappear in the half hour as often happens. In the race back there is only silence. After a while I see, we all see, waving across the sky, a beam of light: right, left, right, left, like a searchlight, or a lighthouse light warning shipping in the area to beware. This however is a different kind of warning light: it is an air defence projector looking for Shahed (Iranian built) drones in the dark, slowly scouting the sky for what carries a missile to destroy, a missile to kill. As someone in the van said, another day of the Russian War in Ukraine.

Sofia, in a wonderful article, later uses the metaphor for the drones of the wings of swans beating as they ascend. But these are no swans. These mean destruction. Too often death. Death in the form of swans' wings beating.

Right, left, right, left...swish, swish, right, left.

Back and forth, back and forth, illuminating above us, searching through darkness and rain. Back and forth.

Eventually we pass where the air defence projector is located. I cannot see it in the dark, but the light suddenly disappears, no longer over our heads, but behind us.

And we are in Kyiv.

I learn later that a Shahed drone had made it through the defences and exploded into a man's house in Chernihiv Oblast, not far from where we had driven through, about an hour after our own departure.

Yes, indeed another day of the Russian War in Ukraine…

*

I am driven to the hotel I had stayed at in Kyiv, where my bags were held whilst I went north. I am not good at goodbyes, so quickly make my exit. Sasha has to return to her flat in a different part of the city. We hope to meet up at the train station but she is not sure she will make it. I bid quick farewells, quick thanks. I had already said quietly in that PEN Mercedes people carrier how grateful I was to have travelled with them, that what I felt about it went beyond words.

That I would not forget.

I do not forget.

And thus I disappear. I grab my bags and walk quietly, unnoticed, the eight minutes to the metro system. I still have a ticket, so quickly descend and catch the metro to the train station, having more than enough time make the underground connections.

The train station as always is heaving. A security official thinks I look rather suspicious, demands to see my ticket as I am loitering for almost an hour whilst awaiting the train number to be posted. Finally I learn what track I am to depart from. I go up the escalator to the concourse and down the steps to the waiting sleeper train.

I again travel in a first class cabin with one other berth. The companion this time is an older military man. He does not say much but realizes I have no clue how to put the sheets over the mattress on the bed at my side of the cabin. I suppose I often reek inexperience in the insignificant things, as well as the significant. He kindly helps me to get sorted. I make contact with Sasha on my phone; she has made the train, so we arrange to meet in the central hall in Lviv in the morning, as it is already pushing midnight. I work on the computer for a while, watching Kyiv starting to disappear behind. I begin my way journey south, and west. Back. Back to… I cannot be sure.

There is much of which I am no longer certain.

18 March
The Road Home

In the morning, Lviv.

I meet Sasha in the main hall as scheduled. I have time. She asks if I want to go to her flat to wait, but I prefer to spend the couple hours getting something to eat, waiting on my own, seeking out the bus that will take me from Ukraine back into Poland.

I do have a gift for her.

I had intentionally given away all of my copies of *A Requiem For Hania* in the weeks before, but I had kept one that I had marked up with post-its as the copy used for readings in Colorado two years previously. I remove all these post-its, clean it up, and give it as my weak but heartfelt offering. I do not know that she, or indeed any, will ever read this book. I do not know if it is worth anyone reading. But the book was essential to understand my journey into Ukraine. It is thus a gift that speaks volumes from within; it means something to me to pass it on to her.

Sasha had been my translator these last days and has become a friend. I truly hold her close inside of me; it is hard to impart, hard to part. She has managed, like the others, to scribe her way into my conscious memory and quiet heart. I hold her, as my other friends, close. And it was important to me that I give what mattered so much to me on this journey, on this longer, long, necessary journey, to her.

*

It only takes a couple hours on the bus from Lviv to the border, driving through countryside, a bus barely filled with a few older people, mostly a few women. A young man at the back, keeping to himself. Wearing fatigues. And me.

It gives me time to think, this Eastern European Bus Lines old creaky bus. It gives me a time of quiet. Time to reflect. Looking at the countryside, passing through a few western Ukrainian villages, untouched, seemingly far from this war. Much to consider. Much to contemplate.

After those couple far-too-short hours we reach the border crossing at Medyka. The wait at immigration for the bus is long. Everything is searched. All passports must be carefully checked.

Finally the bus driver tells us to get off the bus at the Ukrainian passport control building, an old warehouse like structure, to go through immigration there. We stand in line, wait. Finally a large woman in a military uniform calls me forward. She looks at my passport, at me. 'Volunteer?', she asks. A corner of my mouth slightly breaks into a smile: at my age, what could I volunteer for? No, I answer. 'Tourist?', she asks. I am not sure what that means. War tourist? Was I that? Was I more a volunteer? How could I explain my presence? How can I explain, really explain, to anyone? How to explain that I was a 'Voice' tourist—looking for voices, for words. For me. For others.

Because words matter so.

Because voices matter so.

Because the young, like the old, need to witness, and to speak, and to laugh and to cry and to care and live. And die. And live.

Who would understand that?

Yes, I answer. And again, thinking now as I write this. Yes.

We reload the bus and drive the one hundred fifty meters or so to the Polish immigration building—and the entrance to the European Union.

Here we again wait for some time, until we are ordered inside. I watch as the Polish military border guards give the bus a thorough going over. Inside the building, I wait until I am called forward, first putting my bags through a scanner. For me the questions are largely a formality: I am on an EU passport and consequently have freedom of movement. It is a simple how long have you been in Ukraine, where are you going, what have you been doing? I am careful to keep my US passport well hidden. I had carried it with me in case of emergency, although never needed it. Into the EU it does not offer freedom of travel; the questions about dual citizenship may be more extensive. I do not want to answer the questions.

The young man who had sat in the back of the bus follows me through to the waiting officials. He wears military clothes I note again, unmarked of insignias. When he had shown his passport on the Ukrainian side, I immediately noted the passport was not Ukrainian and thought it I saw, correctly, its British seal. There he was asked his purpose in Ukraine, and he said volunteer. They let him through.

The Polish side—the EU side—was not so easily crossed. As a British citizen he is no longer in a citizen of the EU thanks to Brexit.

He also wears military clothes. When he grabs his bags the German Shepherd sniffer dog goes fairly haywire. The young soldier volunteer, not being EU, then had much explaining to do, and every inch of his backpack, everything in it, is inspected, opened, queried. I do not know what set off the dog barking. It is possible the young soldier once had some drugs in his backpack; that would not have surprised me. It is possible there were some remnants of a smell still there. Or an explosive smell. Firearm smell. The Polish border soldiers find nothing, but open everything. They take a knife and cut open a package sealed with tape, possibly a gift. There is nothing.

After they finally, reluctantly, let him through, as we all wait for the inspection of the bus to be completed, I go over to the young volunteer to ask if he needs help sorting out his things again. He is perhaps surprised to hear an English voice speaking to him; I think he is pleased, rather than relieved.

We stand talking, and carry on talking for a bit on the bus, where he resumes his seat in the back. He is from south London, twenty-four years old. He had been in the UK military he said. When war broke out in Ukraine, he felt a need to go there. He is a volunteer soldier on the front. I do not ask if he has been in combat. I know he has. He also says he had had a little medical training—very little, I suspect--and has helped in that capacity in the east of Ukraine as well. We talk about London. He is from south London; I had lived thirty-five years in north London. We joke you need a passport to cross the Thames. We probably mention football; it is a common ice breaker. We talk about the city. He wants to know about my work. I explain I am a writer, that I had travelled with PEN Ukraine to Chernihiv, that we distributed books, talked to people, tried to give what we could through words. Our weapons.

For reasons I perhaps will never know, he is supportive and highly approves. He comments how bad it had been in Chernihiv at the beginning. How so much had been destroyed. How so many had died.

I nod. I know.

I think he is simply pleased to speak to someone in English on the journey home. I think too he is pleased to speak to someone who, frankly, got it. Who too had a reason for having been in Ukraine. Who cares, for reasons sometimes hard to articulate. It is not that he is simply happy to hear an English voice, given his minimal Ukrainian. It is, I believe, that he understands the meaning of the journey. And the necessity to bear witness. Not a war junky. Not the adrenalin rush. But rather the search to understand. To find a way to help, yes. But to find oneself, whether in one's twenties or one's sixties.

I sit in my seat a few rows in front of him. The drive is only about thirty minutes to Przemyśl, from where I first started my journey into Ukraine. I will get off the bus here, catch a train to Wroclaw on the other side of Poland, from where the following day I will fly to Ireland.

I am changed.

I have been appreciated here. No one sits in judgement of what I do. No one says you are good or bad at what you write.

Here you exist only for the time, the fight in whatever way you can, the meaning, the identity, the place.

Here you exist to be.

And to be… the journey.

As we approach that bus station, that train station that symbolizes the end of the time in Ukraine, I stand and walk back the few rows to kneel by the young volunteer.

"Listen," I say to him: "I admire what you are doing. I approve of it. It is a good thing. But I want you to listen to me. You must take care. You must always be careful. You must not die. Not there. Not now."

He nods. He understands. He says he wants to give me a gift and pulls out a military issue can of what I thought was a beer. That night I empty its contents into a sink, as I cannot carry such on a plane, nor put it in baggage under pressure. It is not beer, but rather some sticky high energy drink. I know its military purpose, its military issue. For all I know there may have been a slight 'cocaine' kick in it: keep your soldiers alert, active, do not sleep, move fast, run fast, aim well. Kill.

And live. Do not die. Live…

I keep the can as practically the only souvenir I want to retain, save for a couple small things I had been given in the libraries. Save for some words. Some memories. To me, it speaks volumes. To me, it has value that cannot be explained, but needs to be remembered.

Live: I so hope for this young, young man, who could have been my son, who was younger by far than my youngest son. A part of me goes with him too. A part of me cries for him. Fears for him.

May he live.

*

<u>19 March</u>

Wroclaw is a large city. A western city. It has its charms perhaps. It has its shops, its westernized airs.

I noted but did not notice.

A night in an air bnb near the train station.

A morning bus ride to the airport.

A Ryanair flight, again, back to Shannon airport.

As we descend into Shannon after three hours, I stare at the familiar green landscape that I now call home. The sun shining in spots for a change. The rain taking a short tea break.

I wonder what I am returning to. I wonder what I have left behind. I have no answers. I found no answers. What I found were generous people, a battered landscape, a desire for voices to be expressed and heard, a need to say this is who we are, who we are meant to be. We exist.

When we land I look at my phone. I am still attached to the Kyiv warning website: another air raid in Ukraine. Go to shelters now. Get out of danger. Get out of death.

I have gone to the shelter, and emerged.

I am in the shelter still.

I have never entered. I am still at risk. The missiles still fall. The drones still approach. I am there.

I am safe.

I am not safe. And I will never be safe again.

Again.

I wish I could say more. For the moment I need silence. To process, as I will tell many. To try to understand why in this place, this Ukraine, I had a sense of acceptance and belonging and self that I had not felt in a very long time. Perhaps never felt. I had not needed to justify myself, to explain what I was, what I did, what it meant to be a writer. I had not been judged as good or bad at what I do. I had been isolated, and yet in a funny way not as isolated as I always have felt, and with the war raging in Gaza, with the things I had seen thrown at what I am, born into, isolated in Ireland more than ever.

I needed to return to Annie, my wife, who I dearly love.

I needed too, and still need, to understand the journey I had been on and continue to be on, the search for some sort of meaning. Perhaps I found some answers in Ukraine. Perhaps I did not. Perhaps I felt oddly at home. Perhaps I did not. Perhaps I would be welcome there in different circumstance, perhaps not.

All the answers are not forthcoming. Just the questions.

And the dead, the ghosts, are there. Are here. They whisper to me in a language I share, a language I understand, through them.

At the grave of Victoria Amelina, she who touched me so, I said Kaddish. I was not one normally who would do so. I lay a stone carried from my mountain in Ireland, overlooking the beautiful lake below, at the head of Vika's grave. To say I had been there, that I remembered, that she is of the earth and the earth is within me.

The earth there indeed is within me. As it is here, in Ireland, where I might finally find a short rest. A short moment of peace.

This place, Ukraine, these people have touched me. Perhaps I touched a few in return. They are a part of me. I a part of them. I did not find all the answers I sought. I found some. I found a need and ability to express self. And I found a slight reflection of self on this road, on this journey: now not at its ending, not its beginning.

There I found a bit of hope. A bit of despair. A bit of possibility.

And some voices that will be whispered, and heard.

May they all live to share those voices. May I be one who listens, and grows, and believes.

I am safe. I am not safe. I am safe.

I will never be safe again.

I hear. I know.

II.
The Journal of Emotional Response

This is not a travelogue. I do not write travelogues. It is not a tourists' guide or how-to guide. Rather I paint a picture with words. Images. Faces. Impressions. Emotions. A journey of self and soul as I have said elsewhere.

A Requiem For Hania brought me here. A book. A character who has taken over. And pushed me in a direction I need follow.

So a journey into what some may call the heart of darkness. But it is not dark. Rather melancholic. Beautiful. Pained.

I had some time ago recognized my need to go into Ukraine. The novel I am working on, *Fragments,* ends at the border between Poland and Ukraine, during the influx of refugees at the start of the full scale invasion of Ukraine by the Russians that began on 24 February, 2022. However this journey, whilst I wanted it to focus on my time through the length of Ukraine, in truth begins in Krakow, in particular a short time spent at the former, and indeed current, mental hospital of the Babinski Institute in Kobierzyn—now a suburb of Krakow.

The Babinski Institute had played a large part in the story of *A Requiem For Hania*. It plays a part too, for different reasons, in *Fragments*. I had wanted to write about an almost non-character from *A Requiem For Hania*, Waleria Białońska, in this next book: Waleria, who would be the sole patient to survive the exterminations of the SS at Babinksi. Thus I felt the need to visit this hospital where she had lived, and escaped, indeed just as the fictional 'Hannah Kielar' had lived, and arguably been reborn.

But the visit proved to be extraordinary in many ways: necessary, illuminating, deeply affecting. Looking at it now, I realize it was the start of this personal journey that led me to, and into, Ukraine. Every bit as necessary. Every bit the need to bear witness: to the past, as well as the present.

*

<u>2 March</u>
Kobierzyn, Krakow

The ghosts whisper loudly in my ear here. Thunder in thought and memory of what happened The ghosts of imagination. The ghosts of those who were real, of those who were once here. Who died here, from here. I still feel their tears running into my own. Their fear. Their confusion. And there was most certainly confusion amongst those already confused, and lost.

No comfort.

I have come this way to see the crossroads of the imagination and the historic truth.

To the Babinski Institute.

In *A Requiem For Hania,* in this place, the mute, war-damaged character Hania Stern, then become Hannah Kielar, is brought in 1946 by those who do not know, who never know: for care, for analysis, for help. Perhaps for life. She arrives in silence. Does not speak. Hears but not does not respond. Hers a fiction. A world of fiction that in my ears, my mind, becomes all too real.

Here too Hannah Kielar as she had become meets a doctor who will become a lover and husband, Kazimierz Palinsky. From them a story of life is born, of memory, of redemption, of identity. Of what is lost, what is found. A story of the Warsaw Ghetto, and an antisemitic Warsaw of 1968, and a story of a present day Warsaw: that Warsaw where finally silence and memory meet in a granddaughter's discovery, that granddaughter Agnieszka.

In truth, it is my story, and my journey. Fiction and fact meld into one.

And that journey has brought me here, to this place, seeking not only the imagination that emerged in that previous journey, that previous novel, but in this present undertaking: *Fragments,* a continuation of what I sought in that first book. Not found then. Seeking now.

I have come looking for one who survived, in history survived, Waleria Białońska, a real life character made fiction as 'Lera': an innocent who escapes, she the only hospital patient in reality who did escape in 1942. Thus Lera, who in my story had once fallen in love with a young boy her age, a boy only a memory, and who reaches out and somehow touches and is touched by an old Jew from the Pale of Settlement. This my Lera, finding her need and voice in the memory of that old Jew and in the memory of that young boy she once loved, embodied in the gift of a broken violin. Her story as I write it is fiction, but I cannot help but wonder myself at this crossroads between fiction and truth: what then was real? What was not?...

*

A guide has brought me here from the centre of Krakow. We wander into the ground of this now dilapidated, crumbling place that was once a grand sanitorium for the ill and mentally displaced. Part of it functions still as a mental hospital, but most of its many chalet-like buildings are silent.

But for the ghosts.

I hear them. They reach out to me to take my hand. They, like me, seek redemption. Redeemed from history, and fate, and loss. The seeking. The journey.

At the entrance from a wide, four lane road, through the gate and along the long drive leading up to the first primary building, I see a farm building/gate keeper's house some one hundred fifty or so meters away. I know this place from history, where on 22 June 1942 the head of house of this hospital would wait in his rooms in this small building for a phone call that might come—it does not—and would watch as the almost six hundred patients remaining would be taken from their various wards, in various buildings, by the SS, and led to cattle cars that would in turn take them to Auschwitz. And extermination.

I know where we are. We are at the first whisperings of death. And a death camp for the mentally ill. I hear them even now, frightened, confused. I hear them.

We walk up the long road in silence. At the end, a circle drive in front of what was once the theatre, the entrance to this factory of health and hope. I recognize all as I have seen so many photographs. It seems familiar in so many ways. Perhaps too familiar.

The theatre is empty now. Closed. No concerts. No music to play as it did more than eighty years ago. The normality that was once has now become the normality of empty buildings. A historical site with a history that few if any might remember. Care to remember.

We wander far into the grounds of the large estate, staring at mostly empty buildings, low, part collegiate campus almost, part welcoming small chalet dormitories, offices, clinic: welcoming in their simplicity, used no longer.

I know there were Jews here. They were removed in the autumn of 1941. All taken to another home for the mentally struggling, the mentally too unfit to survive according to the Nazis, taken up to a different hospital in Otwock, near Warsaw.

I have been to Otwock. Hannah Kielar, born Hania Stern, lived the imaginary last days of her life in this town, listening for the voice of her own ghost. Her lost friend Alicja.

The Jewish patients of Otwock were taken in July, 1942, to Treblinka. Like the non-Jewish patients of the Babinski Institute taken to Auschwitz, they would be marched, uncovered, naked, ultimately alone, into the gas chambers. They would cease to exist. They would be forgotten.

I refuse to forget.

The patients of Kobierzyn, here, in this place, they too disappeared even before the Jews of Otwock, many of whom had once been here. The SS arrived on 22 June, that 1942 summer's day, and marched the remaining patients to the trains. The cattle cars. Onward into oblivion.

Most people now do not remember. Do not know the story. But I remember because a different story led me here. And stories resonate in my head, demanding memory.

We walk through the grounds. Look over the wide, empty farm field behind. I have seen this in photographs too. I know it was worked. It is worked no longer.

From one of the small chalets a man opens a window. Patient or attendant we cannot be certain. He could be either. He is not curious; his face is blank. My guide says we are looking for a monument. He knows of no monument. He is like the many who come here in that unawareness. He says go to the reception building. We could find the hospital reception I know, but I have no desire to ask there. The hospital still functions as such and they address the present, not the past. Not the imagination of a writer. Or the latent, subconscious memories of a Jew.

We wander and eventually we find the memorial ourselves, hidden behind another building. Of little consequence. Memory has little consequence, for most.

Three sides to this memorial. In the centre, a cross. Pray for them. On the left, in Polish, the names of all the patients taken, exterminated. On the right, in Hebrew and in Polish, a list of names of all the Jews who had been at the hospital before there were transported to Otwock, almost a year before that awful day of 22 June, 1942 when the remaining patients of Kobierzyn were forcibly removed to the camp at Auschwitz. One month later those Jews would suffer the same fate as did those patients here in Kobierzyn, when from Otwock they were pushed into cattle cars of a train that would carry them to the gas chamber of Treblinka.

I look at the names, one by one. I place my fingers over them. The surnames are familiar. I grew up with names like these, from school, from synagogue. Perhaps there were relatives here. Relatives in the diaspora. One does not know. But few now would know at all. Would seek out.

I fear my voice, my memory, too is dying out.

I leave some stones at the base of these names. I quietly say Kaddish. I quietly remember. I know that as I disappear the next generation, and the one after, will not know. Will have no memory. Will see only a curiosity, or will see nothing at all.

But I, I still hear the whispers. The whispers of ghosts.

We wander further. We find one of the crumbling chalets, its windows largely broken, its crumbling façade largely covered by protective fencing. We try the door, find it unlocked, enter.

Broken glass. Crumbling plaster. Rooms that shout memory. Here patients lived. And died. Here a bathroom, the sides of a large bath still upright. The pipes from long ago from disappeared plumbing fixtures remain still in evidence.

Up a broken staircase, more rooms, a corridor, silence. A half collapsed rusted gurney. Some collapsed metal bed frames. A dormitory of memories.

In *A Requiem For Hania,* in just such a space, there is referenced an empty blue seaman's trunk from a photograph I had found of this place, in a room such as this, at this hospital, in a derelict, abandoned building. There is no trunk here now, if there ever was in this particular building, this ward. In *Fragments* that trunk is central to a story: it holds a hidden broken violin, called memory: that memory of an old Jew from the Pale, that memory taken, protected, worshipped by a young innocent Lera, Waleria, she who becomes the guardian of memory.

As am I, the creator of a fiction, the one who stands here in silence, knowing history, hearing the cries and whispers of this painful history.

I am touched in ways too difficult to explain. Emotion abounds. And emotion unbound.

Eventually we wander on, saying little. We slowly start towards the front entrance of the park, for it is as much park as it is sanatorium or hospital, far in the distance.

But first we come to the chapel. It too is now closed. No service of remembrance here, and if there would be, what would be remembered?

I walk up the stairs of a covered portico. The door is locked. I turn to the side and note now, on the inside of the porch protected from rain, a large brass memory plaque.

The plaque honours one who survived. Waleria Białońska.

My Lera. My Waleria.

I am in shock. I am incredibly moved. I reach up, touch the words. Waleria Białońska. I know you. I remember you. I have created a fiction around you to honour you in my own way, a character whose simplicity, and honesty, and decency, and love speaks volumes to me. Whispers in my ear. Ghost tears from her to me.

She survives still.

Across from this memorial in this portico, another brass plaque, honouring the nurse who on that day of 22 June, 1942, with the complicit knowledge of the man in the gatekeeper's cottage to whom Waleria—my Lera—had been a maid, honouring that nurse who had helped Waleria to hide. Finally to escape. Hidden. Alive. The freedom to live. She did escape: the only patient from that terrible time, this terrible place, who would live. That nurse, that sister nurse, was Stanisława Pałys. She too I would fictionalize. She too I would remember.

She too I would thank, in my imagination, in reality, would remember and thank. And honour.

I know her too. I am touched, and was touched. I remember. I may be alone in remembering but memory demands that I do not forget.

I look around part in amazement, part from my heart as well as my head. I have borne witness here. I came for something that I have found. Truth, perhaps. History, perhaps. But something more. Something deep within me.

We quietly, wordlessly, leave the grounds of this massive place, this hospital, now disappearing from time, from memory. The pain and the love. I feel great love for this place, knowing what happened here. Not love for the events and of deaths, the whisperings of loss, but for those who allow my imagination to give light to darkness. For my Hannah, my Hania, who in my imagination rediscovered her Voice here. For Waleria and Stanisława who lived, and live within me, within my Voice, my need.

I know, leaving here, that this is the beginning of the journey that I have to make. But in fact it is a journey that I have long been making.

I am looking for the past. I am looking for the imagination. I am looking for words, and story. I am looking, too, for an often painful present, in a war now waged, that others may not disappear.

Mostly, I am looking for myself.

*

4 March
Lviv

The crossing of a border in an old Soviet era train. Passport taken then returned. Why are you here? You should not be here. I am here to meet with writers I respect. I am here to tell them their words are my words. I am here to tell them that those before me were killed simply because they…were. And I need some here to know that I am with them. Not simply solidarity. Everyone who comes here speaks of solidarity. I am here for that, but there are other reasons as well. A section of a new book. A section of needing to understand, again. A section of a search. A life searching.

A train cabin shared between three of us. A gorgeous girl—gorgeous because she is full of potential. Of life. Yulia. Living in Bristol. From Ivano Frankivsk. Returning back to Ukraine on holiday to see home. And a 59 year old soldier who has been on holiday. Valery. He speaks Spanish. I work at my Spanish, weakened by time and age and lack of use. Yulia acts as translator from Ukrainian to English when necessary; it usually is. We communicate. Valery is returning to the army. He fights. By trade a landscape gardener. Now he fights. And dreams of retiring from the army next year. And no longer having to fight. Or die. He does not plan to die. He looks at a copy of *A Requiem For Hania* and says that he too wants to make a mark. Leave something behind. Not behind I want to say; before you. What you leave is your grandchildren: their memories. Their love for you. That they stood with you, laughed and played and sang and dreamed—with you.

His thirty plus year old son has been called up. The son has a family, a business, others depend on him, but still he has been called up, although this father is already in the army. Is one not enough, Valery asks? Is one not…enough.

I too have sons. War should be fought by old fools like me. Not the young with lives before them. Old fools.

Yulia. A paralegal. Trained as a lawyer here in Lviv. Maybe she will become a lawyer in the UK one day. She dreams of travel. Just beginning to travel in her life. The lives here were not really like that…before. Not a world of privilege. A world of dreams to make real. But then stopped somewhat by Covid. By a war. A gorgeous kid who could be my kid. I am lucky, I tell her. I could have been born here. My grandparents came from here a long, long time ago. But I am lucky. I had the material trappings of growing up in a middle class United States. So fate would have it. It is only fate.

In her dorm as a student, she tells me, one hundred fifty boys. The cream of their year. Bright, eager men and women. To change a world. Their world. Now eighty percent have been killed. What am I supposed to say to that?

I tell Julia to visit us in Ireland. I give her a card. Come stay. My grandparents taught me the lesson: always a plate at the table. Always a bed. So come visit. What I do not say is that her youth, her need, her loss—gives me a sense of need as well. To reach out.

The countryside is beautiful. The apricot trees are not yet in bloom. Waiting. In Ivano Frankivsk I should visit the Carpathians, they say. Go hiking. One day. Not this day. One day when the war is over.

The sun sets over churches with roofs of silver and gold. The houses are basic. The land is all. They are home. They are glad to be home. This is their…homeland. They both say so.

I am not home. I am looking still.

What homeland means. I can never go home. I have spent a lifetime trying, but you can never go home again. I know. I am.

When the war is over. For all of them. All of us. My war never over.

The train finally arrives in Lviv. I can only wish Valery good luck. Luck is not enough. I want to tell him do not be a hero. He wants to give something back. I cannot tell him what he has to give back is what he has to give to his grandchildren. Not his life. Not his blood. His life he should give to his grandchildren. I fear…And Yulia I hope to see in Ivano Frankivsk, where she is headed, where I will go to meet young writers. To have a coffee with this bright young woman. To tell her that her hope, her faith, has weight.

The weight of water is great.

At the train station to meet me, a writer who I had 'met' online, and for whom I was lucky to be able to do a favor: picking up a train ticket for her in Vienna just in time, between trains, carrying it to Lviv a few days later. She is a very fine writer. A brilliant poet. Iya Kiva. Award winning. She joins me in a taxi to the hotel. A little time to talk. Why did you write *Hania*, she asks: a story of the Holocaust? It is that, I tell her, but only in part. Because it is a journey I began. And I continue on the journey. Because I am a Jew. And I seek to understand. Because the ghosts speak to me. And I need to answer to them. Because. Just because.

So I am in Lviv. I am silent. I will not be silent. Words will push me on. Words are my weapon. They have brought me to this war. They have brought me here. This is who I am.

And who I have to be.

5 March
Wednesday

You would think there is no war. You would think nothing changes. A city much like Vienna, Paris a bit, Krakow a bit. But secret places, hidden places abound.

A morning spent in conversation with Maryana and Taras at the Lviv Cultural Institute, at least that is what I think its name is. I will learn later it isn't, but that is close enough. Maryana and Taras assisted Natalia Romik with her work on the research and exhibition 'Hideouts' that I had seen and on which had attended a conference in Warsaw two years earlier. Natalia inspires much of my new work *Fragments:* a character, an arc, a dig into the present seeking the past, a rebuilding in words, story, theme. Maryana and Taras also assisted Philippe Sands with his *East West Street* work. Philippe, who I first met thirty-five years ago. And who now speaks to me in words and story as I too look into the dark worlds of genocide and crimes against humanity.

So we speak of hideouts. Of secret places. They direct me to the story of the Chigers, hiding in the Lviv sewers for two years to escape death from the Nazis. A story well known. I did not know, however. They tell me about a sequence of caves in the north of Ukraine where others hid for two years, moving from passage to passage, total darkness when the oil light goes out.

Total darkness.

They tell me about the ravine of the Janowska forced labor camp just at the suburban edge of Lviv. And the extermination point for many. Many. Another. I have been to too many. Now Janowska is a prison. That in its way has not changed, although thousands are no longer executed there. Exterminated. You cannot enter now. But the ravine is there for all and no one to see. Eighty thousand people murdered there. Shot and pushed into this ravine. Later this year they will begin unobtrusive archaeological examinations. They will look for ghosts but will try to let the ghosts remain untouched. Unseen.

The ghosts however are never really untouched. And untouching. They are there still. Only a small monument stone remains for them. In their name. In their tears. Yet they are still heard. In this secret place. This hidden place where they did not hide. This hidden place of loss and pain.

They give me the route movement of the Chigers along the subterranean sewer system. Tell me how some citizens helped them by dropping in food. How they were not found. But almost found.

Along a central street in the old town I later walk from manhole cover to manhole cover. Below ground they remained, just here. Above ground I walk, tracing the passage. Tracing the past.

A tram passes over the past. No one knows what was, once, below them, now, below them. But I know.

Secret places. There are secrets then, as now. Hidden places to uncover. Darkness then as now. Hiding in hideouts. Hidden.

The hidden recesses of the heart. And the fears. And the need to survive. The secret paths below and above. I have come to bear witness. I bear witness.

<u>6 March</u>
Grey, rainy morning.

For twenty-five minutes I walk quietly up to Luchakiv Cemetery from my hotel. I wait at a closed gate, looking through the vertical bars of a long iron fence at the populated, chaotic headstones so reminiscent of Pere Lachaise in Paris. I remember strolling through Pere Lachaise so many times, when Paris was my home. That was almost fifty years ago. A life in Paris seems a lifetime ago. So it was. This is a different life.

While I wait a short funeral cortege appears, bringing a body not to the cemetery, but rather home. The home that was Lviv. To a church, a house, a funeral home, I do not know. A place to mourn. To begin to mourn. Many will mourn. Several police cars make a guard of honor as the hearse and a few other cars pass along the way. From every car that waits in every direction the drivers turn off their engines and emerge. They bow their heads in respect. Everyone does the same. I know the cortege carries a soldier. How old was he or she? It is painful to consider. A boy? A young girl? A life extinguished in a war he or she did not want? Martyrdom here is respected. But such loss is still loss.

I am told that in some cases people get on their knees in respect as a body is carried home…

The young woman I am waiting for, Sofia Cheliak, arrives, indifferent to the drizzle. Waves. We have been communicating for some time now. She is a PEN member and I had asked for someone to bring me to the grave of Victoria Amelina as the labyrinth of Luchakiv is huge.

I had followed Victoria Amelina—Vika—since the beginning of the war. She was a very good writer. Well respected. Her story is known to so many. Owned by so many.

But to me she was something—important. She had joined a group of others to report on war crimes. She had been the visible face of what was being lost. A young woman with a husband, child, she knew she took risks. She was driven to do so. And for me, like me, she was a writer who knew she had to bear witness. To know. To remember.

She visited Ireland a couple times on behalf of PEN, reading to children, telling her story, telling others' stories. A beautiful life.

I was to meet her at a concert for Ukraine late last summer in Dublin. I had wanted to give her a copy of *A Requiem For Hania* as a gift. It too is an exploration of what it means to bear witness. My parallel journey. Needed. Necessary. But at that concert there were too many people and wires got crossed, so I just missed her.

We sent the book in a roundabout way to Ukraine. It felt important to me to do so. Her own journey as necessary as the emotional journey in the book. As necessary as my emotional journey. And hers.

Probably a few days, hours, who can say, before she would have received it, she took some South American journalists to bear witness, to explain, to Kamatorsk. As they sat having dinner in a local pizza restaurant a missile struck.

Victoria Amelina did not survive. She would never read *Hania*. She would never know the words of that different story, yet not so different. Her journey ending. Mine, frozen in pain.

Now this lovely young woman, Sofia Cheliak, Victoria's friend, has offered to take me to her gravesite. She explains to me that Vika could not be buried in the site for martyrs, the soldiers, because she was a civilian. The authorities had made the decision. So they put her remains in a slightly different place. Victoria had at first wanted to be cremated, but then thought she would like to buried in this cemetery. She got her wish. Others wished she hadn't, not in this way. At this time. I am one of those others.

Her grave then, not far from the entrance. The mound of dirt not yet settled after these many months. A headstone will follow in time. For now a cross. And flowers. I add mine to those there. On behalf of PEN Ireland. On behalf of writers. Sofia places a small plant she has purchased in the mound itself. I stand there for a long time, looking down at the large round picture of Victoria resting with the cross. That innocent, so very wise face, beautiful, calming. And the toy stuffed unicorn. She loved unicorns.

She chased unicorns. I chase unicorns.

I ask Sofia if I might do three things. The first is to read a poem. Sofia assures me Vika would have liked that. So in the slight drizzle I read W.H. Auden's 'Stop All the Clocks', or 'Funeral Blues'. It too speaks in its way of loss. The pain of loss. It speaks to me. It speaks to the rain.

With Sofia's permission, I then do two other things. This is very much a part of why I have come to Lviv, indeed Ukraine.

I say mourner's Kaddish for a woman I greatly respected. I am not a religious person by any means. But it was important that someone say Kaddish for Vika.

And I lay a small stone at the grave of Victoria Amelina, as is the way of my people. The way of Jews. Sofia wants me to put it at the head of the grave, beside the unicorn. A stone I purposely carried from Ireland. We do not usually leave flowers. We leave stones. That is our tradition. It says: I was here. I remember. I, you, are of the earth and to the earth we return. And last an eternity.

A few years ago now I placed stones at my father's grave, my mother's grave. Now here.

I explain to Sofia why I am doing this. Later I learn that, after a trip to the United States, Victoria Amelina had brought Sofia a gift: a copy of Allen Ginsberg's poem 'Kaddish'. Ginsberg too was the descendent of those from Ukraine, from Lviv. So he dedicated his poem to those here who had come before him. Sofia translated the poem from English. But she had never heard the actual Hebrew words of the prayer Kaddish spoken, only the poem. To her my recital thus meant something important, something unexpected. Something of value. The Hebrew words of Kaddish heard for the first time.

Thus Kaddish was spoken. And a stone was left. And both Sofia, this lovely young woman, this friend of Victoria Amelina and this friend to me, and I turned and left in silence, with tears in our eyes.

At PEN events in Ireland, Victoria often is honored with the 'empty chair'…the notion that one of those we support, believe in, cannot attend. So we honor their spirit. In absence.

I honored hers with a stone, and a poem, and a prayer in Hebrew.

Later that afternoon I wrote to my colleagues at PEN Ireland to say what I had done. That I had left flowers at a grave on their behalf, because Victoria Amelina had meant something to PEN Ireland, and meant something still. But that I had done more. I had left a stone. I had recited Kaddish. I knew they would not understand this, so by explanation, I quoted from *Hania*. This is in part what I sent to them as explanation, and the explanation for my journey into Ukraine:

From *A Requiem For Hania*

"There was a second request. Pawel, like so many of us, had been to so many funerals over the years, particularly these last years. Thus, the nature of growing old. That is never easy. He said his other request was that we today say Kaddish for him, the Mourner's Kaddish at his passing. Kaddish in the Jewish liturgy has been said for a thousand years. It is a prayer that praises God. But it also is a prayer to honor the deceased. It reflects on life itself. On tradition. And most of all I think for

Pawel it reflects on family. To say Kaddish is an act of kindness. An act of remembrance."

"Pawel's lovely Warsaw family told me how they had visited their mother's grave with Pawel, an act of remembrance. Of thanksgiving for them and for him. Agnieszka told me quietly how touched she was when Pawel left a stone he had picked up at Treblinka days earlier, how he placed this stone on her Grandmother's headstone. I explained to her, as Pawel would have known, that this is part of our tradition. For us, we do not leave flowers, as flowers are temporal. Rather we leave small stones at a grave. Those stones that we place on a headstone or nearby suggest that we are all of the earth, where life is short and long at the same time. The stones say we remember all our lives and beyond. That we were there and that the loss of a loved one will be part of our memories forever."

I come to Ukraine as an Other so as to voice my support, my respect, my hope and belief in the humanity of these gracious people. And I reflect that in Ireland, these last five months, such like voice in my ears has grown painfully silent.

I will now travel the length of Ukraine, often accompanied by my friends here from PEN Ukraine. I will offer to them my embrace, my words, my voice. And I will bear witness.

To all of you, I send regards

Greg

I will hold Vika within. I will think of her journey, what it meant to me. I will carry that thought in the years that come, this journey, others.

For Vika, Kaddish was said.

8 March

In the south of the country, foot of the Carpathians. Ivano Frankivsk. The war here seems far away—on the surface. My new friend Iya Kiva, a poet, when here some time before, wrote very movingly of the war below the surface, the abnormality that resides even here where time is held in abeyance in the faces of the families, in the eyes of the fathers and the mothers and the children who will have no choice but to remember. In the faces of the lost ones, a lost generation.

She is right of course. 'What does war look like?' she asked. 'Christ, Mary Magdalene and Mother of God who walk the Ukrainian land somewhere between death and life' her conclusion. I will see Iya at the launch of her new book of poetry in Kyiv. I will not understand the words of her readings. But I discovered yesterday, in the reading here from Taras Prokhasko, a well-known magical realist novelist, that you do not have to understand the words to hear the music, the rhythms of language and grammar in sentences. They too have their own context and syntax.

And the faces of the audience.

It is something I worked with in *Hania*, not always understood. Sound. Sound of words. The language of music as the language of story. Repetitive notes becoming repetitive story with slight diversions and changes of tone or direction.

I am here for a festival of young writers, organized largely by PEN Ukraine. I am meeting young writers whose talent and potential and indeed hope speaks to me. Today I will speak with them. I have carried small token books in English for them as gifts. Irish writers to whom language, and how it was used, was everything: Yeats, Beckett, Joyce and I added some copies of a novella by Claire Keegan because, for her, every word is weighed, and weighed again.

The whispers and weight of water. Ripples on its surface.

They have made me welcome here. They seem pleased I have come. It is easy to come here to say I wish to show solidarity. But it is more than that. Something deeper. It is a cry to say you must survive, must give voice. Voice is everything.

I meet PEN Ukraine president Volodymr Yermolenko. Philospher, writer journalist. Wonderful, brilliant man. I heard him speak with Philippe Sands some time ago online. His thoughtfulness is balm. And I meet festival curator Ostap Slyvynksy. A soul mate in his need to bear witness. A poet who lost his words when the war started; instead he began to collect stories from the refugees at Lviv train station and so doing wrote his book 'Dictionary of War'. Because he knew stories matter, words matter. He too has borne witness.

He too I understand, and hold within.

I am welcome here. I am not home, but they are within me in their words, their journey, their refusal to lose hope. Voice is indeed everything. Here there is voice.

9 March

How do I speak about these wonderful young writers I have met here in Ivano Frankivsk? How do I explain how touched I have been in meeting them? How I will carry the thought of them home with me, will carry it far, held tightly?

They are within--me. Their gifts, their kindness, their warmth has been something to behold. And something to struggle with.

A young woman who looked to be fifteen but had to be older, yet still barely beyond a child, a face as sweet as summer wine as is said, came up to me this morning to thank me for coming here, to tell me that my words had meant so much. And she explained that just a few months ago, her husband had been killed in this awful war.

I could only embrace her and not let her see how upset I was. She perhaps was twenty, twenty-one. How do I answer this? To her? To myself?

As I was getting ready to leave, a young one I had not yet met also came to sit with me. To tell me stories. How she had gone to Montana—Montana!—on work experience, living in a small town, working as a hostess in a restaurant. How she loved the mountains, those same Rocky Mountains that just south of Montana had once nurtured me, once called to me. That still do. How she had loved the mountains, more than the sea, the forests. How she had been happy there.

And she tells me about her father. He had been a lawyer. She too did a second degree in law but thinks she wants to write.

Her father had tried to impress upon her that she must play by the rules, must understand the regulations. I did not want to say to her that that is so that one can subvert the same. And challenge authority. And ask questions. The lessons I have learned. I have always felt a need to subvert. To question. And knowing also as I know that until the Orange Revolution here almost twenty years ago and the Revolution of Dignity some ten years ago you could not challenge authority. You had to play by the rules, obey the regulations. I could not tell her. For her, her father was right.

It was then, however, she told me that when the War had started here, really started almost ten years ago in the Crimea, her father had joined the reserves. Because it was the right thing to do. Because in his heart he felt it was the right thing to do, despite regulations, despite rules.

And soon after he left…he too was killed.

And she needed to tell me how difficult it had been for her, because it had fallen onto her to go to the morgue, to identify her father, which she had to do by his teeth.

How do I respond to this? I do not know how to respond to this. But I know I have to listen. And care. And make certain she understands that I care.

Stories make us human.

She said it left a huge void within her. I told her that that void will never go away. That it will get easier. That she will move forward. But that the void will always be there, and she should temper it, hold it, not let it take over but rather carry it with knowledge, and quiet grief, and ultimate strength, because this I know. This I know.

Stories give us our humanity.

She asks me about other war zones. Are they the same? I have to say yes, they are the same. Maybe the armaments change, the sophistication or lack thereof, the denial of human rights sometimes worse, sometimes better. But for the ordinary people, those who simply want to see their children grow, and laugh, and cry, and prosper—yes they are the same wherever the conflict. Because people have the same dreams everywhere.

And still I do not know how to respond. Except to tell her I would listen. And she could find me if she ever wished. And her words would matter. And that she must push to find her Voice, whatever that might mean.

I truthfully did not really know how to respond. And I could not let her see how upset I was. And I could not let her see eyes gloss over, my own tears that wanted to fall. And yes she touched my heart, so that I will carry her, and these other young people, with me.

Bearing witness is something that is important for me. Necessary. But oh so difficult. Oh so necessary, and oh so difficult.

*

I leave them behind, these wonderful, kind, young writers who have touched me. I will never leave them behind.

10 March
0630 Sunday morning

Crowded. Like a crowded airport terminal.
Gift shops and fast food stands between stairs down to railway tracks.
Filled with soldiers. Men and women. Most young.
Moving with purpose. An entirely different feel to Lviv and Ivano Frankivsk.
Here you sense a country at war. Not the front line. The front line is far. But yes here you know things are not normal.
Here there is war.
Welcome to Kyiv.

10 March
Later

The park that is now Babyn Yar.
Here almost 34000 Jews were murdered in a huge ravine on 29-30 September 1941. Over the period of the occupation, as many as 150000 killed—Jews, intellectuals, prisoners, Roma.
The ravine was eventually filled by the Soviets: rubble, flooded, mud. It disappeared, and did not disappear. Still the ghosts.
People out for a Sunday stroll. Some acknowledge, some pass by.
I stand before the menorah that is the primary memorial, the primary remembrance. Through the trees a speaker plays a quiet beautiful rendition of Avinu Malkeinu. Slowly sung. Over and over. I know the words well from long ago. High holy days services with my parents. They too are gone. From within these words memories appear. Memories of a mother, a father. Their faces within me. Their loss within me. I see all the way to their graves. The gravestone the shape of a tulip. The names engraved. Dates. Me.
Stones on a grave.
Hole in my heart. Loneliness.
I leave a stone too at the foot of the menorah. I say Kaddish once again because I have come to remember. To say I was there and have

not forgotten. I said it for my parents. I said it for Victoria Amelina. I say for the thousands. I wonder who will ever say it for me.

A woman with a baby carriage walks slowly past. Glances, then away.

Today, far away, a world away, a Ukrainian documentary, '20 Days in Mariupol', deservedly wins a best documentary award at the American Oscars.

Today, hostages are still held by Hamas in Gaza.

Today, the beginning of Ramadan, Palestinian children, women, mothers and fathers continue to die in that horrible war. And starve. And cry. Another horrible war.

You think I do not hear? You think I do not feel? You think?

There are tears everywhere. Here in Ukraine. The Middle East. Sudan. Over and over the litany of pain. Those desperately trying to escape the poverty of their homes to get to Europe and never getting there, drowning in indifferent seas.

You cannot take the pain of the world upon your shoulders. But sometimes you have to take the pain of the world within. See it. Witness. To say Kaddish is to remember.

This journey itself is Kaddish.

11 March

I meet with a filmmaker I know who is helping another documentary maker, who I also know, about the rape victims of Russia's invasion. It is a very tough subject I understand all too well from my own Bosnian work.

The documentary filmmaker was a lovely young woman I met in Sarajevo a year ago, when she showed her film about a group of kids from the Donbas. Her film touched me hugely, because her kids, there in the film—they were just kids. Like kids I had met everywhere. And in end titles there was a comment on screen that the two teenage boys featured had disappeared after the Russian onslaught. The likely meaning of that did not pass me by.

It still does not pass me by.

The filmmaker, Alisa, had also been in the Ukraine military. Captured. I only learn now that she too was a rape victim. I had not known that at the time. You could say it is none of my business, not relevant. But never was it more relevant. I drop my eyes in thought and sadness.

Two air raid sirens, short lived. An announcement over a loudspeaker in my room at 00.28: go to a bomb shelter. I do not bother. Know it will be short lived. Having trouble caring if it is not. I do not expect missiles here at the moment.

Always expect the unexpected.

12 March

Air raid sirens again, now during the day. No one takes notice. The children in school, however, have no choice. The classroom becomes the metro station.

So, the PEN van meets me at my hotel for a journey I had requested. To see. To understand. To witness.

Bucha, Irpyn, Borodyanko. Maxim and Anna my guides. Burned out buildings. The street in Bucha where bodies lay dying. The house of culture shelled. Mortar holes on a football field. Apartment blocks burned out, destroyed. One block where there were three: now only wasteland to the right, to the left. The river crossing at the Romanaky Bridge, destroyed, a monument to those who made it and to those who did not. A graveyard of burned out cars, the torched bodies of men, women, children no longer within. Modern sculpture of burned out dead. A teddy bear left as a gift on a shattered windscreen whispers quietly. Remember me, remember this child…

The newspaper reports tell what happened in these places. They are now largely rebuilt. How does one rebuild silence, emptiness? A great deal of emptiness remains.

In the town of Borydanko, in front of the severely damaged cultural centre and library, a towering statue of Taras Shevchenko, national poet. Through the statue's head, very visible as a memorial, a high velocity bullet hotel. A Russian gift. The Russians were, are, terrified of words. Of poetry. Of independent thought. Of Ukrainian identity. Words are weapons, weapons to destroy the Russian onslaught. The hole through metal is both a remembrance of trauma past, and a symbol of hope. They can kill, but peoples' thoughts they will never destroy.

Returning to Kyiv later, a poetry reading by my new friend Iya. It is all in Ukrainian. I do not understand the song; I understand the music. This is what she writes to me after: "One of the topics was a language of body as a before: Babylon language. And if we can understand each other without a natural language. Your presence was like an illustration."

Words I know, I hear, I see, do matter. Sometimes so do the silences. And the gestures. And the glances. And reaching out with a hand of support even if words themselves fail.

Earlier in the day we left Bucha through checkpoints, everywhere, always. I stared at the hedgehogs. I wondered if They will return.

They will try to return. They. But they—they—will never defeat. You cannot defeat thought. The weapons of this war that I understand, words, poetry, cannot be silenced. Or destroyed.

But I know too the war is not over. It is a long way from being over.

14/15 March
Final night in Kyiv.

A book reading for killed writer/soldier Andrii Hudyma. Writer, chef, father, husband, bon vivant, sailor, gourmand.

His book *69 Spices of the Heart*.

His daughter, Yulia, opens the reading speaking with warmth, drama, a twinkle in her eye. Hope. Love. She reads of rosemary. It is the only word I can understand.

But sometimes the music touches you, when you do not understand the notes. This has become my constant refrain. And I was touched. I could not let them see how saddened I was hearing his words, the stories they told of this man who in his photograph has the mischievous expression of one who loved life, who grabbed it, shook it. Added spice. Filled not the stomach, but the heart. So I quietly left immediately after the readings. This was not my place. The spices, however, filled the senses. Filled the heart and the belly with anguish and with love. And with humour. Humour mattered, I know. This man touched many. This man touches me.

Yulia, his daughter, is a special young woman. I see her face before me long after I leave the room. A daughter one would have been proud of. He was proud I have no doubt, and would continue to be proud. If he had lived.

He lives through her.

A hole in my stomach.

A hole in my heart.

The final lines of Andrii's book: "No work is worth a second if it is not seasoned with the main spice described here. Love to cook. Love life."

The night, early morning, filled with occasional air raids. But I have eaten well and tasted much. I too have tasted lives here. And I carry that memory of spice on my palette and my heart.

Life is normal. But not normal.

15 March
Friday

Heading north. We cross the 'border' between Kyiv and Chernihiv Oblast (district). Seven others in the van, ferrying books north. The side of the van says Write To Exist. I wonder if it should be exist to write.

We are stopped by the police for speeding—eight km over the limit. 340 kha to pay. $10. Even here the police wait for speeders. That makes me smile, just a bit. A shamus, my father would have said. Watch out for the shamus.

But everything spoken is in Ukrainian. I find myself often isolated. Do not want to allow myself to feel such but I am nonetheless. So I stare at the scenery. Burned out trees. Empty farmland. Checkpoints. The Russians destroyed this province. Have to wonder about why. What was accomplished? The Ukrainians refuse to disappear. They will fight this existential fight. Existence. Determination.

The roadblocks.

The sandbags and the hedgehogs. Your ID please.

Pass. We have weapons: words are weapons. Books are weapons.

We stop in the village of Yagidne. More a hovel than a village, and every house here is damaged.

To one side of the village, a village of trees, woods, stands what was the village school. The story here is known. The international press came, left.

Here, for 27 days—I prefer now to write this as a number, not in letters (more power in the number)—and again, 27 days, in late February 2022, all the townspeople were forced to stay in the cellars of this small school, whilst the Russians remained above ground in the school, using it as their command centre. Holding the Ukrainians—men, women, children, babies—as human shields.

Three hundred fifty people kept in these damp, small underground dark rooms for 27 days. Ten people would die in this cellar.

The locals do not want to return here. But we in a way have no choice.

We are taken down by Ivan. Red eyes not from crying, but from being there. From witnessing. He survived here with his son, his two grandchildren, now 11 and 15. We walk through the rooms. At each door frame, a number written by the Russians to say how many were in each room. On the walls, graffiti, sometimes drawings by the children. The remnants of their stay remain, each carefully marked and numbered for cataloguing the war crimes. Here graffiti counting the number of days. Here a school lesson, of sorts. Here a cartoon-like drawing to try to ease a child's mind. Here the potties, the torn papers, the stools, only a couple. Most people had to squat in the damp, crowded rooms. Privacy: none. Death: much. This was, and is, torture.

What happened here?

Nothing for the villager prisoners to do but sit on but the torn sofa, the couple chairs: wait, until the leg sores made standing itself painful.

Waiting, almost nothing to eat. No toilets. No sunlight. Often no light at all. No hope. And above the hate. 27 days. For us, imagining, for Ivan, lived, living. Never leaves.

We stare, observers, writers who must reveal. We see still the few bodies finally allowed upstairs, finally allowed to be buried. Shallow grave. Those digging: shoot at them for fun. The fear.

It is hard to describe what I see here. Hard to hear the ghosts, the tears that were here only a short two years ago. Hard to see the pain etched on Ivan's face. In his eyes, his reddened, pained eyes. Hard to know. You have to know.

At one point men from the cellar were taken outside, told to dig a large hole. They assumed they would be shot here. They assumed it was their time to die. It was not their time to die. Where have I seen this before? Too often in the woods of eastern Poland, in Ukraine.

Babyn Yar.

The past now returns. Never again but again and again.

Three hundred fifty people. A mother whose milk ran out for her newborn, who with others pleaded with the Russians that the infant needed milk or would die. 'So it will die;' came the reply; 'this is war, isn't it.' This is war.

They were given food coated with diesel, so they could not eat.

They remained in the dark without batteries.

An old woman dies. Who says prayers over her grave? Throw her into the former kindergarten. Let wild dogs feast.

Who says Kaddish now?

Auschwitz; I have been there. This is different. This is today. This is what they did. This is what they are still doing. This is hard to take in. To see. Need to see. Eyes wide open. With wonder at such hate, such evil.

And children. And the children...

A long time spent in this cellar, looking at the graffiti, staring at the damp floor where these people were forced to sleep, breathe, live, shit, cry: the remants of minimal rations they ate, the bits of clothes left behind, the empty chairs, the damp, the football pitch drawn on the wall to try to make life return in their imaginations, the damp again, the lack of hope, the dim light, the cold, the stifling air, the smells, the ghosts there, all around, those who died and who lived but died inside themselves, the despair, the pain, all around, Ivan, all around, the grandchildren who will remember because they do not forget what happened, what happens, what still will happen. Ivan's red eyes...

When we leave, I shake Ivan's hand, ask to translated for him: look after your family, I say. Look after them. All that is left.

27 Days.

This is hard.
This is war. Isn't it. Isn't it...

*

Then travel on. Libraries. Generosity. Souls that rise above. Humanity revealed in the face of the inhuman. May it not return.

But it may return.

My friend Sasha posted this note about our travels, with a photograph of the PEN Ukraine members, and one PEN Ireland member, sitting at a table laden with food. Hospitality takes on new meaning. The humility and gratitude I feel overwhelms.

Dr Sasha Dovzhyk
'In north Ukraine, locals are desperate to feed @PenUkraine If you think of the manmade famine these villages went through under Stalin & recent Russian siege when they were cut off medical and food supplies, this hospitality acquires tragic overtones. 30 km from Russia, Novhorod-Siverskyi'

16 March
Saturday

A race down mad roads in Chernihiv region, only a few miles from the Russian border. The Russians here attacked, passed through, laid siege to the pretty city of Chernihiv, devastating the edges of this place. Seventy percent destroyed or damaged in these suburbs.

The roads in this van remind of Mr. Toad's Wild Ride at Disneyland. But this ride is not with joy. The roads are destroyed mostly by lack of repair from use, and equally from the dozens of tanks passing by, destroying tarmac, hedges, trees. Bridges blown up. Checkpoints now every so often, soldiers looking in windows, making sure we should pass. We pass.

We visit several libraries, delivering books in Ukrainian, in English. The wonderful writers with me talk about a book they randomly pick from the stack we bring. Why the book matters. Why culture matters. Why these people matter. And they read some war poems from a common anthology they carry with them. It sometimes includes poems written by Victoria Amelina. I do not understand the words, but I understand the message. Again I do not hear the notes of these songs, but I hear the harmonies and melodies and the music itself. And again I am touched. And again I am saddened so that I pain.

We visit a library in the town of Mena. The people here are desperate to hear the words from these books. Desperate to hear voices from beyond this world of war. Desperate too to show off their lovely library, with its sections for children, adults, computers, news, events. It matters so much to them. It is the centre of their world, this place. It gives them hope. It gives them meaning.

They are desperate too to tell their stories. Of how the Russians invaded and were there for more than a month. How some people succeeded in escaping, when they could escape. How this town, surrounded by water and rivers, attracted others from villages, arriving in boats. They thought they would be safe. Where they could be safe. One woman with twin newborns arrived in a boat with an infant held tightly in her arms against each breast. She would not let go. She would never let go.

A film about the Russian invasion, but without subtitles. So I am invited downstairs, where low and behold two locals are singing English and Irish songs in honour of St. Patrick's Day. When I walk in they are so pleased to play a reel just for me. They are so pleased that I am there. I am there in ways they cannot know, representing an Ireland that does not always remember, that sometimes looks away, but more perhaps a U.S. that might as well be on a different planet right now. Ireland refuses to endorse sending bullets. The U.S. right now will not pay for new missiles, for defence protection against the incoming ballistic missiles and daily Shahed drones. Survival, far away, is simply a word; here it is daily breath, and daily bread. Give us our daily bread. Few where I grew up would understand any of this. Whilst Congress debates then ignores this tragedy in Ukraine, refusing to allocate funding for arms, funding for defence capabilities, people die daily. Blood on their hands does not wash away but they are silent, oblivious. Indifferent really. They do not know. They can never know.

No member of Congress, no government official, stands beside me staring into Ivan's red eyes, or feeling his deep, deep pain.

But I am here. And that means something. Something to these people. Something more to me.

And this time, this library, these two delightful, wonderful people serenading with a tin whistle and a guitar, this time I understand the song, the music, and the words are within me. I do not forget. I will not forget.

*

As I review these words, and edit, I note the photograph sent to me today of a woman sitting on a park bench in Odessa with her small white dog at her side, enjoying the spring day, enjoying the moment. She will not realize that the incoming Russian missile holds cluster munitions, one of which will strike at her feet. Will she feel the explosion as the munition blasts and strikes? Will she feel the shards of hot metal, the pain? Will she know before she falls?
And then see the subsequent photograph of her bloodied body lying on the ground, the twisted remains of the white dog beside her.
Just a woman sitting on a bench.
Welcome to the images of this war.

*

Another library. Two young girls desperate to talk to me in excellent English. To tell me they love Ireland because of the sit-com 'Derry Girls'. They befriend me on Facebook, on Instagram, girls who could be daughters if not granddaughters. They so want to take a photograph with me, one arm over the shoulder of each girl. And with the others from PEN. They want to be seen. They want to be remembered. They want to be girls. They want to exist and for those on the 'outside' to know that yes, they are, they live, they love. They simply are.

A final stop. Final library. But here the reception is different. Tension in the air. We will 'go with the flow', see what happens. Not read or recite but watch. We are taken to the cellar. Only adults here. Anonymous, expressionless faces. And the librarian who smiles only slightly. Most sit against the wall away from the long table in this rather damp cellar. Unwelcoming. They give little away, their stone stares, their apparent lack of curiosity, particularly the hard man at the head of the table. He is a large man, strong, the look of a mafia godfather about him. Looking at us with a somewhat wary, indifferent eye. He welcomes us, but the welcome is cold. He is a deputy leader on the local council I am told.

So we begin to talk. And it is clear that I will be asked to speak as well, to explain what it means to be in Ukraine, to listen to stories, to bear witness. My friend Sasha acts as translator. I say that it is necessary for me to know, but also necessary for people to see that they are not forgotten. That they matter. That words and art and music matter. And I say that it is the day before St. Patrick's Day, the most important holiday in Ireland, where we celebrate our words, our music, our song, our dreams and yes our independence. That I say is what I bring to Ukraine, and what I see in Ukraine. What I dream for here in Ukraine.

Here in Ukraine. Here.

The comments touch understanding. There is nodding, and some warmth. A man stands and reads a poem full of patriotism and strength. We are thanked and some smiles. Then we are taken upstairs whereas always hospitality is generous, and yes I share some vodka with the politician. We clink glasses. I know him. I know who he is, what he is. I know too that in truth, he wants the best for his family, his friends. His town. And I, I will not be cowed. Because despite the bravura, I know he too has suffered, and does not want to show it. Friends and family and school mates and those he knows, lost, dead, forgotten.

There are lessons I learn later. This town, like others, was occupied for weeks. It is still very close to the front line. They still fear and fear drives them into the cellar where they are safe. We are safe. Where we will not be seen by those who strive to see with hard hearts. This town: there was damage...but more, these people feel abandoned, and forgotten. It transpires we are the first artists to visit this place since the 1980s. For practically forty years they have felt alone. All they had, their culture, their television, their music, their lives dictated by a Russia just across the border. There. But they are not Russian. They are Ukrainian and plant their stake. Say their names. Say their identities, their selves. Say who they are.

But who has listened? Who is listening now?

Their wariness is understandable. How do I speak about solidarity, when solidarity is in short supply? In Ivano Frankivsk I thought about a lost generation. I remarked upon it. Here I find just the lost. Seeking to be found. Desperate, angry to be found.

And the hospitality that they have laid out, the cakes and food made, the vodka poured—Sasha reminds me that these people have suffered so and have very little. So it has been since the time of the Stalin famines of the Thirties. Starvation and death. We are not that far away from such starvation, not really. Yet they share with us what they have, because we have reached out, because at least those amongst us want to care. And because we say we will return one day. I wonder if there will be a return. It is a question I cannot answer. It is in my heart, but I do not know if it will ever be in my power.

Or if they will be here should I return.

The councillor's grasp when I shake his hand is strong. I understand men like this. I know the Achilles heel. I know the man. And I know beneath the bravado there is righteous anger, the anger of feeling alone, abandoned, lost on a bigger stage and not being able to do much about it.

I take his hand. I look at him and nod. I will take his hand, yes.

17 March
Sunday

It is St. Patrick's Day. One last excursion to a library, but one that is different. Perhaps we were not expected, but there is a holiday here. The women are dressed in local embroidered costumes. There is a performance later that we cannot stay for. The library itself speaks of money and offers great support: play areas and a trampoline, a room with some caged rabbits and guinea pigs for the children, books, a blood pressure monitor, small exercise areas, a theatre. A library very well endowed. The head librarian shows us around with unbridled enthusiasm—before she has to disappear to join the other like-dressed women for the performance and to give out food from the now all too common spread.

One area is worth mentioning. It is where the 'coffee ladies' would gather perhaps to sew or embroider. Except here they are making camouflage netting for the troops. That is what they darn and sew and 'embroider' these days. That is the statement. They too know, occupied for forty-two days. Everyone knows in their hearts that safety is fleeting. The library is a refuge. The one at the edge of town did not survive. Knowledge, the community is everything. Everything.

They embroider camouflage netting. I think about that. I run my fingers over it. Hiding from all that has happened. Like so much, it speaks volumes. It speaks of strength. It speaks of intent. It speaks of a people who do not give in, never give in. It speaks too, however, of a fear of what may come. And the need to fight, to hide. And to live. This is not lamentable. But it is sad.

Then a rush back to Chernihiv city. A tour of the medieval monuments by a young man dressed in medieval costume replete with wooden dagger and sword. I do not understand the words as we walk around this Unesco site that is slowly decaying. Some things are explained to me later—particularly how the Russians have tried to ambush the truth and story of the place. Imperialism offers no surprises.

A stop for a bottle of Jameson, because our group has to celebrate. We raise a small toast to St. Patrick. To the spirit that makes us free. To friendship. To hope…

And then a concert. Two women singers who are national heroines, and a full orchestra with them. A wonderful concert to celebrate the life and death of Taras Shevchenko, national poet, writer, hero. His words, their music, their patriotism. Their belief. The concert is stirring, the music often beautiful. Afterwards we join the conductor and singers who have been to Ireland and loved it. They travelled around singing. Sligo choirs. A singing competition. They did well. We raise glasses again. We wish the producer happy birthday. We drink some whiskey. We celebrate.

And I am touched. Again. These people. This kindness.

*

Then the final drive back towards Kyiv. I have a train to catch: trains, buses, the journey home. It is time. It is hard.

As we drive, the usual air raid alert. But a bit different this time. We leave in darkness, with an alert in the Chernihiv Oblast. An hour or so after we pass through, a missile hits the district just where we were. A family house destroyed. Another family left with nothing. And as we hurry towards Kyiv, we can see the anti-aircraft search projectors/lights moving from right to left above us, looking for drones. A drone that delivered that missile to Chernihiv. The projector light right, left, right, left, right, left.

War is never far away.

Remember that. Always remember that, and when I return to the safety of my home in Ireland, the safety of London, the safety of my past, remember that some need now to survive, and to fight for their future.

And for some, some so very young, to die for that future. I struggle with this reality and am no longer certain where my reality resides.

18 March

This will be the final entry. I may add more later, or not. I cannot give in words what is within. But one final story.

The overnight train to Lviv. In my first class sleeper an older soldier. We do not really speak other for him to show me how to place the blanket within the fitted sheet cover because I am rather a naïve fool.

Then arrivals in Lviv. 0600. Await a bus back into Poland. But first a book passed as a gift to my fellow traveller Sasha, sometimes my translator and now my friend. She is someone special. I want her to have this copy of *Hania*. I want her to remember me. I feel strongly that she, that others, should know of my journey of many years that has brought me here. I will hold her in my thoughts: her kindness, her friendship. This is friendship I have rarely known. She is setting up an institute in Lviv, having left teaching at Birkbeck in London. Hers is a fine, sharp mind. Like all the writers and intellects who travelled with me north and left me humbled, often silent, and yes very very much in awe.

So finally my bus journey back to Poland.

At the border we are held for a long time. Both sides: Ukraine and Poland. The EU. Passports carefully checked. On the Ukrainian side I am asked if I am a volunteer. I smile and say no. I am too old to fight I would like to say. So tourist, she asks? I guess I am. But I hope not a war tourist. That is not why I have come. That is not the journey I have taken; it has been far more personal than that. Far more necessary.

Or maybe indeed I am a volunteer, fighting as I know how, with words and heart. A volunteer who witnesses. And who volunteers a bit of himself, leaving that behind.

On the Polish side the transfer is a bit faster. Except for one young man who is dressed in solider fatigues and who I quickly ascertain is English. The sniffer dog has started to bark at him, so everything of his is searched. Every single thing. Cutting open packages. Opening the smallest container. They shake him down for a long time. Perhaps he had had some dope residue in his bag, or perhaps the residue of gun powder. Who can say.

When this is over, we start to talk. He is a Londoner, and a kid. Really, a kid. He was in the military at sixteen in the UK. When the Ukraine war started, he came to Ukraine to volunteer. He is twenty-four now. He has been in the country for two years, on the front lines. A kid. He is friendly. Full of his own kind of bravado, a quiet confidence. We exchange stories: who we are, why.

A kid.

I am getting off at the first town where I will catch a train to take me to Wroclaw, then a flight home. As we approach I go to the back of the bus to say something to this young, brave, in fact kind young man. This soldier who is twenty-four now but older. Older than I am. Older and younger and alive. I tell him that I admire what he is doing. It is a good thing. But I tell him please, please…stay safe. Just stay safe.

I want him to live. He hopefully will. He may not. I want him to live.

I want him to have a life.

Stay safe, my young friend. Stay…

Safe.

III.
Two Letters that Matter

A letter sent to my Uncle, to cousins, that needs inclusion

30 March 2024

Dear Uncle Buni, Dear Mark

I had thought of disseminating this in a Dinner family email but have decided not to.

I know you sometimes put out farms' newsletters; if you wish to do so there feel free; it's as much really for your information/interest I think as not. Others may be interested; many will not.

*

As some will know I have quietly spent a few weeks in Ukraine in Feb/March. I had hoped at one point before going that I might be able to travel to towns associated with Grandma and Grandpa: Buzaky, Ratne, Ustyluh, Teklyne, Kovel…These towns (Kovel is a city) are largely in the Volyn Oblast—district—in Northwestern Ukraine sandwiched between Lviv, Lublin in Poland and Belarus to the north…thus a major district, Oblast, of the Pale of Settlement which was the beating heart of Ashkenazi Jews.

However, I was unable to go there this time, partly because I cannot speak Ukrainian or read Cyrillic, partly because of the war. Whilst this Oblast has avoided much of the destruction and fighting that has happened/is happening in other parts of Ukraine, including Lviv to some degree, it simply would not have been safe enough or easy enough to travel on my own. There are live minefields in so many places and without a fixer it would not have been wise, especially as many of these villages are so close to the Belarus border from where the Russians and to some degree Wagner group entered Ukraine, and indeed, confirmed by locals I met, Belarus soldiers as well.

I did spend some time in the north of the country at the oblast further to the east, Chernihiv, within 30km of the Russian Border.

I do not wish to go into my movements in Ukraine here, but Chernihiv, like Volyn, indeed like all of Ukraine, is both wooded and agricultural, replete with cornfields, wheat and other grain fields and at times with echoes for me of the Greeley world of Grandma and

Grandpa. In Chernihiv Oblast I saw no livestock; I am not sure that cattle were a big part of the world there. I did see large farmland of corn and wheat. A picture is below of one. Much of the crop, however, was burned out by the Russians, as were grain silos, with equipment taken and many houses/farms destroyed. Perhaps some livestock killed as well, I did not ask—because too busy documenting the men, women and children who were.

I had said to Uncle Buni once if I could find any records /information I would let him know. To be honest, even despite the war, there are few records to find. Whilst there are online records of Jewish communities in many villages if you search, much in hard documentation has disappeared under the Soviets, let alone the Holocaust. Most synagogues are such no longer. If they stand they are used for different purposes and not recognizable for what they once were. Jewish graveyards, often on the outside of villages/towns, have often become overgrown, or disappeared entirely. They tend to be ignored or forgotten unless overseen/restored somewhat by overseas Jewish organisations. Although Jewish communities can be found in cities, in smaller places that is usually not so. A friend who runs Holocaust Awareness Ireland told me a story a few days ago: someone he knows was in a small town in Ukraine some time ago and asked some young people if they could direct him to the Jewish cemetery. In fact they knew where it was. What these young people did not know was what had happened to Jews there or what the Holocaust was...Thank the Soviets for that. And of course the Holocaust itself.

Despite its reputation for antisemitism in the past, I found nothing but kindness, graciousness and great dignity amongst all the Ukrainians I met—and I met many. As said I do not want to discuss this journey right now, but I very often made it known that I was Jewish and was always met with decency and friendship. As a passing note, I will be hosting/doing a talk q&a with a major Ukrainian writer here in Ireland in June, who won a Canadian based Jewish prize for her last major book that in part looks at the loss of the Jewish community from Ukraine and seeks to explore and deepen the relationship of communities. The woman who wrote this book, Sofia Andrukhovych, is a friend; she is not Jewish. Her book is being translated into English and will be published next year by Simon & Schuster. It's a breakout book, not just about the Jewish community but about the loss of intelligentsia in Ukraine under Stalin; it looks as if the US publishers are going to try to push her as a new Elena Ferrante in some ways. If interested let me know and I will try to signal when it is released.

I also spent time in Poland—this time in Krakow for work purposes. That is a different conversation, not part of this email, with slightly different reasons for being there. Sometimes. But it is interesting to mention in passing: a couple years ago I met and was helped in Warsaw during a conference at a museum for an exhibition of another friend's work (I put in here the link to her work, because it is fascinating. Called 'Hideouts', my friend is an academic historical archaeologist, and the exhibition dealt with hidden entrances, recreated in silver cast for the exhibit, where Jews hid from the Nazis in Poland and a bit in Ukraine….)

https://zacheta.art.pl/en/wystawy/natalia-romik

The young woman I refer to above, a friend, is working on a project to digitalize and archive every matzawot—headstone—that can be found in Poland still if not in the graveyards that remain. As you probably know, during the war the Nazis destroyed most, pulled them up and used them as paving stones, concrete fodder, repairs to buildings and farms, anything to erase the Jewish population from history. It is an interesting side note and Klaudia, my young friend, has a difficult but necessary task ahead of her (I think they are looking for research funding if anyone interested…)

Whilst I had hoped to send you photos and descriptions of a world that has largely disappeared in Ukraine, alas I am not really able to do so. However, a final couple comments in passing. I often referred when asked to my grandparents coming from the Volyn Oblast in a very different time. As I explained, I was not and am not an all too typical American looking for his 'roots'; that is not my way. However I have been curious about many things…not so much place, as what hides inside. Who we are rather than where we come from. Despite the remark made a few times, with regards to food, I now know why all my Grandmothers made potato pancakes or pickles or borscht--or or or--in such a way…and now understood how the recipes came about, my motivation for this journey was not and indeed is not to look at this idea of 'roots'.

However there is a moral, ethical world handed down to me, within me, that was learned, taught without words but by deed, action, within DNA perhaps. This I saw in Ukraine. Metaphorically it may best be demonstrated in what I said over and over to the many who have become friends: if you are ever able to make it to the UK or Ireland (and painfully young men cannot leave the borders except by special agreement), there is always a bed at my house, always a plate at my table.

That is the lesson that has been handed to me. Unspoken, but very much a part of the DNA handed from all my grandparents.

I send regards

An open letter

To all those in Ukraine--writers, filmmakers, young writers, local people, artists-- who have touched me more than words can say:

18 March 2024

An open letter to all at PEN Ukraine,
To those young writers from the Ivano-Frankivsk,
To the villagers and wonderful people of Chernihiv Oblast,
To the filmmakers in Kyiv and
To the wonderful people who took me by the hand in Lviv:

As I slowly make my way west back towards my home in Ireland, it is you, and Ukraine, that is etched in my memory, on my heart, in my thoughts.

What you have shown to me is immeasurable kindness, generosity, strength of spirit and hope. I am humbled at meeting so many of you and witnessing only decency and warmth. I truly am at a loss for words.

I take back west with me a bit of each of you inside. I take back memories that will last a lifetime. I take back friendship that will hold me tightly forever. I take back your hope for a future that will bring you peace, and may that be soon. I take back your creativity, your words, your images, your music. I take back you.

I simply want to say thank you to each and every one of you who sheltered, and led, and laughed, and drank and helped me on my own journey, helping me to find my Voice. A new friend from PEN Ukraine asked if I intended to write about Ukraine. My answer is complex. Your stories are your stories, there to be told and heard by you, not me. But in your humanity that you demonstrate, this I will take with me and will find its way into my journey.

I look forward to hearing all your voices in the future. I look forward to raising a glass with you all in the cities, towns, villages of Ukraine and I hope in Ireland as well.

I have been deeply touched by my journey in your country. It is a journey that I need to make: to bear witness, to understand, to find in the hearts of all that which gives meaning, and that which makes us human.

I wish all of you, your families and friends, your people only safety and kindness. Be well my many new friends. I carry you in my heart and prayers.

With only and always great kindness
Greg

IV.
Final Word

<u>4 April 2024</u>
Mountshannon, Ireland

It is early morning, 0300, some weeks later, the morning of my birth, some sixty-eight years in the past.

I do not sleep.

I lie in bed, remembering. Go get a cup of tea, remembering. Sit in darkness, remembering. Carrying the journey still. A personal journey. I take it alone.

Final three images that stay with me:
Yulia, the young daughter of the chef Andrii Hudyma who wrote the wonderful *69 Spices of the Heart*. Her face, amongst all, brings me comfort, brings me sadness. A beautiful girl whose father will not give her away at her wedding. Brave in ways that cannot be expressed. Full of belief and life still, but loss. I hold out my hand to her. She more than much else is now etched on my heart, my memory.

Ivan, in the village of Yagidne, leading us into the damp school cellar where in February 2022 the Russians held all villagers for 27 days. A place of death, where some died, some could not breathe, some became hopeless. The graffiti and children's potties left as evidence. He too a prisoner. He too, his family, victims. His eyes red not from crying but from the pain of memory. I left shaking his hand and told him to look after his family. Even now I sadden at this thought. Look after your family, Ivan. They needed you, and they will need you.

And finally I see the air defence shadow-light cutting through the night, tracing across the fog-heavy black sky as we drive back to Kyiv, back and forth searching for death, for defence, for life. My friend Sofia, wonderful writer that she is, likened the drones to swans taking flight, the sound of their wings somehow terrifying, and in the case of instruments of destruction and death, not disappearing. And now in memory, I hear those wings still beating. I still want to run.

And I still seek, as I have on this journey I have undertaken, scouting the skyline in darkness, crouching from the wings, watching the light, searching for one's life, one's death, defying, seeking meaning, seeking self, seeking identity and existence. Back and forth, back and forth, back and forth, back and forth, and back…

*****

***

<u>Post Script</u>
Mountshannon, Ireland
Many weeks later

    I try to process. I do not know how to process.
    I try to speak. It is difficult to speak. I tend to stay silent. To reside in silences.

    Some weeks, many weeks before I left, my wife Annie suggested we both take DNA genetic tests. Curiosity.
    So we took the tests. Sent them off.
    The curiosity inevitably waned. Krakow, Ukraine took over.

    But some time well into my travels, I found an email waiting from her.
    'Your DNA test results have come back,' she wrote. 'You won't be surprised that it says you are ninety-seven percent Ashkenazi Jewish.'

    And then she added: 'You're home.'

    I wonder.

    I wonder.

Acknowledgements and Thanks

And because I need to give thanks:

To Yulia who befriended me on the train from Poland, and joined me for coffee in her home of Ivano Frankivsk. May we meet in Ireland or Bristol where she is a law clerk, dreaming of great things. And to the soldier Valery, aged 59, in the train cabin who is returning to war but dreaming of retiring in a year's time, and who only wants to leave something behind: leave behind yourself for your grandchildren. That is a gift that weighs more than any book.

To Sofia in Lviv who took me by the hand when I said kaddish at the grave of Victoria Amelina.

To the young writers in Ivano Frankivsk. I cannot name you all, but you touched me to my very soul.

To Alyssa who helped smooth that passage in Ivano Frankivsk and welcomed me so.

To Ostap, who ran the festival, who included me and through him I learned that even when the words do not flow, there is testimony to take. His 'Dictionary of War' is a bible.

To Roman, who let me speak about a film I did not love, but the meaning of that film in the context of my own life has weight.

And in Kyiv:

Irish journalist/documentary maker Johnny O'Reilly: kind words, exceptional talent.

My dear friend Marysia Nikitiuk, whose talent is unbending and who will fine her way.

Another film friend, Nadia Parfin, who looks for story and speaks words of truth and power.

And of course the wonderful members of Irish pen:

Volodymyr Yermolenko, whose link to Philippe Sands is a link I respect and so admire. And share even slightly.

The wonderful, generous Tetyana Teren, without whom I would be truly lost, and whose generosity knows no end.

Maksym Sytnikov, who always had a smile, whose strength to preserve (and drive no less) is a gift. Thank you.

Anna Vovchenko, brilliant literary translator, who joined us to see the destruction of Kyiv regions, and who quietly saw me, and led me.

Iya Kiva, who I met in Lviv ferrying a train ticket that I was able to collect in Vienna, but whose wonderful poetry to which I listened, while not understanding the notes, spoke to me in their music.

The wondrous, beautiful Yulia Gumida, young daughter of lost writer Andrii Gumida, killed in Bakhmut, and who spoke so eloquently at the remembrance readings for her father and who brought me to tears, despite saying that no tears should fall. She I will long remember.

And directly, finally, to my fellow travellers to Chernihiv, who not only put up with me, but who have touched me in ways they will never know:

Sasha Dovzhyk
Tetyna Teren
Maksym Sinyelnikov
Sofia Andrukhovych
Myroslava Barčuk
Kateryna Kalytko
and lastly, but not last in any way, Vakhtang Kebuladze

My heartfelt thanks to each of you.

All your accomplishments are too great to list, but what you were, and are to me, I hold as the greatest treasure.

There are more to mention, those who so moved me. You are not forgotten. Rather I hold you within and carry you with me. Mostly I thank the people of Ukraine. Live. Prosper. Overcome. Be—you.

Be alive.

Be.

www.ingramcontent.com/pod-product-compliance
Lightning Source LLC
Chambersburg PA
CBHW061150170426
43209CB00036B/1959/J